GET GOD

Books by Kevin Johnson

Early Teen Devotionals

Can I Be a Christian Without Being Weird?
Could Someone Wake Me Up Before I Drool on the Desk?
Does Anybody Know What Planet My Parents Are From?
So Who Says I Have to Act My Age?
Was That a Balloon or Did Your Head Just Pop?
Who Should I Listen To?
Why Can't My Life Be a Summer Vacation?
Why Is God Looking for Friends?

Early Teen Discipleship

Get God: Make Friends With the King of the Universe
Wise Up: Stand Clear of the Unsmartness of Sin
Cross Train: Blast Through the Bible From Front to Back
Pray Hard: Talk to God With Total Confidence

Books for Youth

Catch the Wave!
Find Your Fit[1]
Find Your Fit Discovery Workbook[1]
Find Your Fit Leader's Guide[1]
God's Will, God's Best[2]
Jesus Among Other Gods: Youth Edition[3]
Look Who's Toast Now!
What Do Ya Know?
What's With the Dudes at the Door?[4]
What's With the Mutant in the Microscope?[4]

To find out more about Kevin Johnson's books or speaking availability visit his Web site: www.thewave.org

[1]with Jane Kise [2]with Josh McDowell [3]with Ravi Zacharias [4]with James White

Make Friends With the King of the Universe

GET GOD

Kevin Johnson

BETHANYHOUSE
MINNEAPOLIS, MINNESOTA

Cover by Lookout Design Group, Inc.

Published by Bethany House Publishers
A Ministry of Bethany Fellowship International
11400 Hampshire Avenue South
Bloomington, Minnesota 55438
www.bethanyhouse.com

Printed in the United States of America by
Bethany Press International, Bloomington, Minnesota 55438

Library of Congress Cataloging-in-Publication Data

Johnson, Kevin (Kevin Walter)
Get God : make friends with the King of the universe / by Kevin Johnson.
p. cm. — (Early teen discipleship ; 1)
ISBN 1-55661-636-8
1. Christian life—Biblical teaching—Juvenile literature. 2. Christian teenagers—Religious life—Juvenile literature. 3. Bible—Textbooks. [1. Christian life. 2. Bible—Study.] I. Title.
BS680.C47 J64 2000
248.8'3—dc21

00-010396

To Nate, Karin, and Elise

May you get God—and grow deep

KEVIN JOHNSON is the bestselling author of almost twenty books for youth, including *Can I Be a Christian Without Being Weird?* and *Catch the Wave!* A full-time author and speaker, he served as senior editor for adult nonfiction at Bethany House Publishers and pastored a group of more than four hundred sixth through ninth graders at Elmbrook Church in metro Milwaukee. While his training includes an M.Div. from Fuller Theological Seminary and a B.A. in English and Print Journalism from the University of Wisconsin–River Falls, his current interests include cycling, guitar, and shortwave radio. Kevin and his wife, Lyn, live in Minnesota with their three children—Nate, Karin, and Elise.

Contents

Part 3: Figuring Out God's Faithfulness

Part 4: Staying Clear of Sharp Sticks

Part 5: Building on the Rock

How to Use This Book

Welcome to *Get God*. This book is part of the EARLY TEEN DISCIPLESHIP series, better remembered by its clever initials, ETD. I wrote ETD as a follow-up to my series of bestselling devotionals—books like *Can I Be a Christian Without Being Weird?* and *Could Someone Wake Me Up Before I Drool on the Desk?* ETD has one aim: to help you take your next step in becoming wildly devoted to Jesus. If you're ready to work on a vital, heart-to-heart, sold-out relationship with God, this is your series.

The goal of *this* book is to help you make friends with God, the King of the Universe. *Get God* prods you toward that goal through twenty-five Bible studies designed to make you think—okay, without *totally* breaking your brain. It will help you

- dig into Scripture on your own
- feed on insights that you might not otherwise find
- hit the heart issues that push you away from God or pull you closer to him.

You can pick your own pace—anything from a study a day to a study a week. But here's what you'll find in each study:

- Your first stop is BRAIN DRAIN—your spot at the beginning of each lesson to spout what you think.
- Then there's FLASHBACK—a bit of background so you better understand what's coming up.
- Don't skip over the BIBLE CHUNK—a hand-picked Bible passage to read.
- You get STUFF TO KNOW—questions to help you dig into what a passage means.
- There's INSIGHT—facts about the passage you might not figure out on your own.
- DA'SCOOP—definitions of weird words.
- And SIDELIGHT—other Bible verses that let you see the topic from a different angle.

The other big questions are, well . . .

- BIG QUESTIONS—your chance to apply what you have learned to your life.
- Each study wraps up with a DEEP THOT—a thought to chew on.

But that's not the end.

- There's STICKY STUFF—a Bible verse to jam into your brain juice.
- ACT ON IT—a way to do something with what you just learned.
- And DIG ON—another Bible passage to unearth if you want more.

And one more thing: There are cards in the back of the book for all the verses in STICKY STUFF, with a few bonus cards thrown in—since we'd already killed the tree.

If you've got a pencil and know how to use it, you're all set.

EXCEPT FOR ONE THING

You can study *Get God* on your own. But you can also work through this book with a friend or in a group. After every five studies there's a page called "Talk About It." Nope—you don't have to cover every question on the page. There are too many to answer, so pick the ones that matter most to you.

Whenever you do an ETD study with one friend or a bunch, keep in mind three goals—and three big questions to help you remember those goals. And nope—you don't have to actually ask those questions each time, because that would feel canned. But each time you meet you want to:

- EMPATHIZE: *What's gone on since the last time you got together?* To "empathize" means to put yourself in someone else's shoes. Galatians 6:2 tells us to "carry each other's burdens" (NIV), or to "share each other's troubles and problems" (NLT). Whether you call them "highs and lows," "wows and pows," "uppers and downers," or "wins and wedgies," take time to celebrate and support each other by chatting through life's important happenings and offering simple, to-the-point prayers.
- ENCOURAGE: *Where are you at with Jesus?* Hebrews 3:13 says to "encourage one another daily. . . so that none of you may be hardened by sin's deceitfulness." Religious rules apart from a relationship with God are deadly. So instead be real: Are you

growing closer to or wandering away from the Lord you're learning to follow? Is anything tripping you up?

- EQUIP: *What one truth are you going to take away from today that will help you live closer to Jesus?* Second Timothy 3:16–17 promises that "All Scripture is inspired by God and is useful to teach us what is true and to make us realize what is wrong in our lives. It straightens us out and teaches us to do what is right. It is God's way of preparing us in every way, fully equipped for every good thing God wants us to do" (NLT). Don't leave your get-together without one point of truth that will make a difference in your life. It might not be the thought or verse that anyone else picks. But grab at least one truth—and hang on tight by letting it make a difference in your life.

Got it? Not only is *Get God* a study to do on your own, but better yet, it can help you grow your faith with your friends. You can pick a leader—a youth or adult—or take turns picking questions and talking through them as your time allows. Just keep the three big goals in mind.

Now you're ready. You can do it. Grow ahead and turn the page and get started.

PART 1

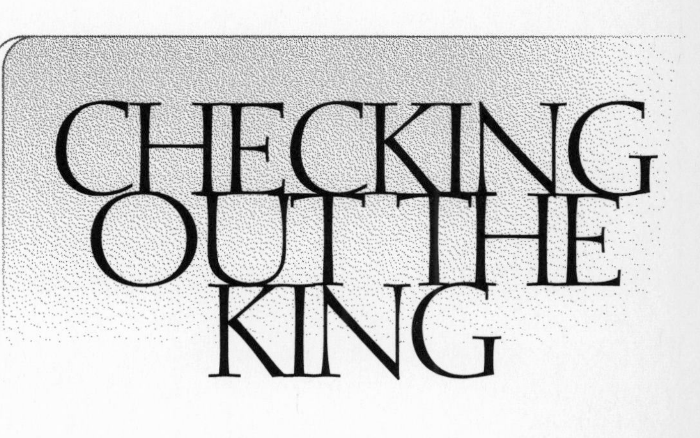

CHECKING OUT THE KING

1. Ka-nock, Ka-nock. Who's There?

Jesus wants to know you

Picture this: You're walking a downtown sidewalk when you round a corner and smash nose first into a street preacher. He grabs you by those little hairs where your head meets your neck. He screams. He pleads. He tells you that you need God.

Even if you never have a close encounter with a spiritual sales-guy of the wacko kind, all sorts of people try to tell you about God. Your brain darts: *Who are you to tell me what to believe?* Or *I already know that.* Or *Sure. I'll listen.* Or *No, thanks.* Even if you've never liked any invitation you've ever gotten to "get God," you need to know that Jesus issues an invite of his own. And he's the one to get if you want God.

BRAIN DRAIN When people try to tell you about God, would you rather have them say more or shut up? Does it make a difference whether the person saying "I can tell you something about God" is a friend—or your parents, church people, or a stranger?

FLASHBACK In this first Bible Chunk you'll briefly meet John the Baptist, a wild guy who dined on jumbo grasshoppers (Matthew 3:4). His job was to announce the arrival of Jesus as the world-changing Son of God. You'll also meet a group of friends who became early followers of Jesus. It seems all of these people spotted something interesting in Jesus. . . .

BIBLE CHUNK Read John 1:35–51

(35) The next day John [the Baptist] was there again with two of his disciples. (36) When he saw Jesus passing by, he said, "Look, the Lamb of God!"

(37) When the two disciples heard him say this, they followed Jesus. (38) Turning around, Jesus saw them following and asked, "What do you want?"

They said, "Rabbi" (which means Teacher), "where are you staying?"

(39) "Come," he replied, "and you will see."

So they went and saw where he was staying, and spent that day with him. It was about the tenth hour.

(40) Andrew, Simon Peter's brother, was one of the two who heard what John had said and who had followed Jesus. (41) The first thing Andrew did was to find his brother Simon and tell him, "We have found the Messiah" (that is, the Christ). (42) And he brought him to Jesus.

Jesus looked at him and said, "You are Simon son of John. You will be called Cephas" (which, when translated, is Peter).

(43) The next day Jesus decided to leave for Galilee. Finding Philip, he said to him, "Follow me."

(44) Philip, like Andrew and Peter, was from the town of Bethsaida. (45) Philip found Nathanael and told him, "We have found the one Moses wrote about in the Law, and about whom the prophets also wrote—Jesus of Nazareth, the son of Joseph."

(46) "Nazareth! Can anything good come from there?" Nathanael asked.

"Come and see," said Philip.

(47) When Jesus saw Nathanael approaching, he said of him, "Here is a true Israelite, in whom there is nothing false."

(48) "How do you know me?" Nathanael asked. Jesus answered, "I saw you while you were still under the fig tree before Philip called you."

(49) Then Nathanael declared, "Rabbi, you are the Son of God; you are the King of Israel."

(50) Jesus said, "You believe because I told you I saw you under the fig tree. You shall see greater things than that." (51) He then added, "I tell you the truth, you shall see heaven open, and the angels of God ascending and descending on the Son of Man."

STUFF TO KNOW

First of all, what's this about Jesus being the "Lamb of God" (verse 36)? Hint: A few verses back John told what the Lamb of God would accomplish when he said, "Look, the Lamb of God, who takes away the sin of the world!" (John 1:29). Why would that impress and interest anyone enough to go see Jesus?

INSIGHT In the Old Testament—the first half of the Bible and the place to learn the story of God's people up until Jesus—lambs and other animals were killed to pay for people's sins, the wrong things people do that offend God and hurt others. What sounds incredibly gory was a flash to the future. It was a picture of how Jesus would die for the world's sins as the ultimate Lamb of God.

Who invites Simon to come and see Jesus? Why (verse 41)? Who invites Nathanael to come and see Jesus? Why (verse 45)?

INSIGHT "The Messiah" was the special servant of God the Old Testament said would come to save the world. "The Law and the prophets" is a quick way to say the Old Testament writings that predicted his arrival.

Nathanael isn't immediately wowed by the invite. How do you know?

What does Jesus do to convince Nathanael of who he is?

Does it work? What does Nathanael decide about Jesus?

INSIGHT "Angels of God ascending and descending on the Son of Man" echoes an Old Testament story (Genesis 28:12). It's like Jesus is saying, "Hey—when I arrived the heavens split open! Now you're gonna see what God is like."

BIG QUESTIONS The chance to check out Jesus

didn't end in Bible times. Another verse in the Bible shows that the invite is for everyone: In Revelation 3:20 Jesus says, "Here I am! I stand at the door and knock. If anyone hears my voice and opens the door, I will come in and eat with him, and he with me."

If Jesus knocked on your head and your heart and said, "I want to get to know you and I want you to know me," how would you respond?

If you could ask Jesus for one thing to convince you he's for real, what would it be?

DEEP THOT You need people to prod you toward God. There's nothing better than a caring parent, pastor, or friend who opens your eyes to God. But you only truly get God when you see and follow Jesus for yourself. Jesus won't grab you by the scruff and shout in your face. The choice to enjoy his friendship—or not—is up to you.

STICKY STUFF Stick Revelation 3:20 in your brain's long-term storage. You can find it on a card at the back of the book.

ACT ON IT Sketch a picture of Jesus knocking. Stick it someplace to help you remember Jesus wants to be friends. Hey—if you don't feel artistic, trace the outline of your own hand ka-nocking. Or a doorknob—you can draw a circle, can't you?

DIG ON You can read about how other people bolted to follow Jesus in Luke 5:1–11 and Luke 5:27–32.

2. The Pizza of Life

Jesus satisfies like nothing else

You'd be way past amazed if Jesus showed up at a football game with a half dozen pizzas and multiplied them to feed five thousand people. And you might be way past bewildered if Jesus then said, "I am the pizza of life. Come to me and never go hungry. Believe in me and never thirst." But if you're like most people you'd want to be in line for Jesus' free scarf-till-you-barf coupons to your favorite pizza eatery.

BRAIN DRAIN What does God have to offer you? Is there anything he *can't* or *won't* give you?

FLASHBACK Before this Bible Chunk, Jesus had just done two incredible miracles. Miracle 1: He was teaching a large crowd when the time slid past lunchtime. Knowing that drive-thru fast food wouldn't be around for a couple thousand years, Jesus took two fish and five loaves of bread, broke them, and fed five thousand people. The people he fed loved him so much they wanted to crown him king (John 6:15). Miracle 2: Jesus had to hide away and catch up with his disciples in the middle of the Sea of Galilee—and no, he wasn't riding a Jet Ski. He walked on the water. The crowds caught up with him on the far shore. They call Jesus "Rabbi," which means "teacher."

BIBLE CHUNK Read John 6:25–35

(25) When they [the crowd] found him [Jesus] on the other side of the lake, they asked him, "Rabbi, when did you get here?"

(26) Jesus answered, "I tell you the truth, you are looking for me, not because you saw miraculous signs but because you ate the loaves and had your fill. (27) Do not work for food that spoils, but for food that endures to eternal life, which the Son of Man will give you. On him God the Father has placed his seal of approval."

(28) Then they asked him, "What must we do to do the works God requires?"

(29) Jesus answered, "The work of God is this: to believe in the one he has sent."

(30) So they asked him, "What miraculous sign then will you give that we may see it and believe you? What will you do? (31) Our forefathers ate the manna in the desert; as it is written: 'He gave them bread from heaven to eat.' "

(32) Jesus said to them, "I tell you the truth, it is not Moses who has given you the bread from heaven, but it is my Father who gives you the true bread from heaven. (33) For the bread of God is he who comes down from heaven and gives life to the world."

(34) "Sir," they said, "from now on give us this bread."

(35) Then Jesus declared, "I am the bread of life. He who comes to me will never go hungry, and he who believes in me will never be thirsty."

STUFF TO KNOW

Insert yourself in the minds of this real-life mob of people. Why are they looking for Jesus (verse 26)?

What does Jesus *want* them to be interested in? Hint: What is "food that spoils"? What is "food that endures to eternal life" (verse 27)? (The "Son of Man," by the way, is a title Jesus often uses for himself.)

The people say, "Yeah? So tell us what we're supposed to do to please God." What does Jesus tell them to do (verse 29)?

And the crowd then says, "Prove that you're from God!" In the Old Testament—back in Moses' day—they argue, God proved himself to their forefathers by showering edible bread (Exodus 16:31). So what evidence does Jesus offer that he is heaven-sent (verse 33)?

Who does Jesus say is the "true bread"? And what in the world does he mean by that? Check verses 33 and 35 to see what this "bread of life" will *do*.

If you think those words of Jesus are hard to digest, you aren't alone. A few seconds later in verse 51 Jesus said this: "I am the living bread that came down from heaven. If anyone eats of this bread, he will live forever. This bread is my flesh, which I will give for the life of the world." When the people heard this, they said what amounts to "Help! How can we eat his body?" Many of the people who had been on his side said, "Too hard! We can't swallow this!" (verse 60). And get this: Many of his followers stopped following (verse 66).

BIG QUESTIONS At Jesus' words, "many of his disciples turned back and no longer followed him" (verse 66). But those who continued to hang around him made a big decision: They believed that the life they found in Jesus far outweighed whatever fears or frustrations they felt in following him. When Jesus asked his twelve closest friends "Do you want to leave me too?" Peter piped up for the rest: "Lord, to what person could we go? Your words give eternal life. Besides, we believe and know that you are the Holy One of God" (verses 68–69).

What do you think draws people to Jesus—what does Jesus offer them?

What do you think of those people who heard Jesus up close and personal and walked away?

So what attracts *you* to Jesus?

What scares you away from following Jesus?

DEEP THOT Jesus offers you nothing less than a wildly deep forever-friendship with himself: In this same lengthy chat with the hungry crowd he said that "everyone who looks to the Son and believes in him shall have eternal life, and I will raise him up at the last day" (John 6:40). Sounds like the man has a lot more to offer than free pizza.

STICKY STUFF Memorize this mind-boggling promise of John 6:35. You can grab a card in the back of the book.

ACT ON IT Make this lesson real by baking some bread. If you don't cook grab a loaf of frozen dough at the grocery store. Eat it hot with a friend to remember that Jesus tastes good and fills you up full.

DIG ON You can read the whole Bread of Life saga in John 6.

3. Hu Nose U?

God knows you totally

So maybe you're right. Your coach really does have eyes in the back of his head. Your sister really is a spy broadcasting your life by Web cam to the world. And your English teacher really has implanted a bug zapper deep in your skull to slap you when you sleep. But sometimes you're still glad when the right person can see right through you: the doctor who can shine a bright little light in your ears or up your nose, the friend who spots your hurts a mile away, the parent who knows your every need. Sometimes you want your privacy invaded. It all depends on who's doing the invading.

BRAIN DRAIN How would you feel if a hidden camera were peering into every corner of your life? Who would you trust to run the camera?

FLASHBACK Psalm 139 was written by David, a man who experienced flying highs and belly-scraping lows in his relationship with God. King of Israel around 1000 B.C., he was both a guy with God's heart (Acts 13:22) and a betrayer who had his loyal soldier Uriah killed so he could marry his wife (2 Samuel 11:15). Even so, he wasn't afraid to have God look inside his life.

BIBLE CHUNK Read Psalm 139:1–18

(1) O Lord, you have searched me and you know me. (2) You know when I sit and when I rise; you perceive my thoughts from afar. (3) You discern my going out and my lying down; you are familiar with all my ways. (4) Before a word is on my tongue you know it completely, O Lord.

(5) You hem me in—behind and before; you have laid your hand upon me. (6) Such knowledge is too wonderful for me, too lofty for me to attain.

(7) Where can I go from your Spirit? Where can I flee from your presence? (8) If I go up to the heavens, you are there; if I make my bed in the depths, you are there.

(9) If I rise on the wings of the dawn, if I settle on the far side of the sea, (10) even there your hand will guide me, your right hand will hold me fast.

(11) If I say, "Surely the darkness will hide me and the light become night around me," (12) even the darkness will not be dark to you; the night will shine like the day, for darkness is as light to you.

(13) For you created my inmost being; you knit me together in my mother's womb.

(14) I praise you because I am fearfully and wonderfully made; your works are wonderful, I know that full well.

(15) My frame was not hidden from you when I was made in the secret place. When I was woven together in the depths of the earth, (16) your eyes saw my unformed body. All the days ordained for me were written in your book before one of them came to be.

(17) How precious to me are your thoughts, O God! How vast is the sum of them! (18) Were I to count them, they would outnumber the grains of sand. When I awake, I am still with you.

STUFF TO KNOW

What does God know about you? Jot a list from Psalm 139.

You'd think it would occur to David that he should run from the roving eye of God. But does David think that hiding from God—from his Spirit—is a good idea? Why or why not (verses 7–12)?

How does God know these things about David—and about you (verses 13–16)?

INSIGHT When David talked about being formed in the "depths of the earth" he wasn't goofed up about where babies come from. It's poetic language for the womb. The biology is clear in verse 15.

What does David think about God's total up-close-and-personal knowledge of him (verses 17–18)?

SIDELIGHT David wasn't perfect. Even though David had reason to hide from God, at the end of Psalm 139 he even invites God's scrutiny. He says, "Search me, O God, and know my heart; test me and know my anxious thoughts. See if there is any offensive way in me, and lead me in the way everlasting" (verses 23–24). He sees God's knowledge of him as the way God could remake his life for the better.

BIG QUESTIONS Of all the people in the world, who knows you the best? What exactly do they know about you?

How does that feel to you?

Harder question: Who knows stuff about you that you wish they didn't? How does *that* feel?

SIDELIGHT There's no hiding from God. He knows everything about you—good, bad, or outright ugly. Cool truth: God sees you at your worst and still loves you. Romans 5:8 says, in fact, that "God shows his great love for us in this way: Christ died for us while we were still sinners."

What do you think about the fact that God knows you completely?

DEEP THOT It's amazing: Do something, God sees it. Say something, God hears it. Think something, God knows it. What's even more amazing is that God uses his all-knowing power for your good. He knows exactly what you need.

STICKY STUFF Fix Psalm 139:13–14a in your mind forever. "Fearfully made," by the way, means you were and are awesome—not that you were scary.

ACT ON IT Go spy on your little sister. Whoops—maybe not. Ask your mom or dad if you've got an ultrasound picture of you in your baby album. How did they feel to see that first fuzzy photo of you? Or what did they feel when they knew you were on the way?

DIG ON Check out Psalm 51, where David comes clean for killing Uriah.

4. I Wanna Be a Sheep

God wants to give you real life

You know people like this: "I'd be a Christian," they say, "except that God would ruin my life." They worry that the God who knows everything is out to use his X-ray vision to smash fun. So here's the huge question: Are they right?

BRAIN DRAIN What's good and bad about being a Christian—what are the pros and cons? Scribble this full:

Pros	Cons

FLASHBACK In John 9 Jesus debated some less-than-kind religious leaders who criticized him for restoring the sight of a blind man. What Jesus proclaims in chapter 10 might not be part of the same conversation, but the contrast between Jesus and the hypocritical leaders is clear. Jesus is saying, "Hey, look. Who you gonna listen to? Those people aren't worth trusting your life to. Trust me."

BIBLE CHUNK Read John 10:1–15

(1) "I tell you the truth, the man who does not enter the sheep pen by the gate, but climbs in by some other way, is a thief and a robber. (2) The man who enters by the gate is the shepherd of his sheep. (3) The watchman opens the gate for him, and the sheep listen to his voice. He calls his

own sheep by name and leads them out. (4) When he has brought out all his own, he goes on ahead of them, and his sheep follow him because they know his voice. (5) But they will never follow a stranger; in fact, they will run away from him because they do not recognize a stranger's voice." (6) Jesus used this figure of speech, but they did not understand what he was telling them.

(7) Therefore Jesus said again, "I tell you the truth, I am the gate for the sheep. (8) All who ever came before me were thieves and robbers, but the sheep did not listen to them. (9) I am the gate; whoever enters through me will be saved. He will come in and go out, and find pasture. (10) The thief comes only to steal and kill and destroy; I have come that they may have life, and have it to the full.

(11) "I am the good shepherd. The good shepherd lays down his life for the sheep. (12) The hired hand is not the shepherd who owns the sheep. So when he sees the wolf coming, he abandons the sheep and runs away. Then the wolf attacks the flock and scatters it. (13) The man runs away because he is a hired hand and cares nothing for the sheep.

(14) "I am the good shepherd; I know my sheep and my sheep know me—(15) just as the Father knows me and I know the Father—and I lay down my life for the sheep."

INSIGHT You've got to understand the sheep pen, a key fixture in the booming sheep economy of Bible times. The pen wasn't a chain fence designed to keep your dog in the yard, but a stone or mud-brick structure or even a cave. It had only one entrance, which the sheep used to go in at night and—you guessed it—out in the morning. Sheep aren't totally stupid, but they need protection and care. The shepherd slept at the entrance to fend off anything bent on harming the sheep—anything with fangs or a frying pan.

STUFF TO KNOW Who are the bad guys in Jesus' sheep story (verses 1–12)?

Trick question: What do thieves and robbers do to the sheep?

Actually, that wasn't a trick question. Both thieves and robbers hurt the sheep—thieves by sneakiness, robbers by violence. This one is a little harder: What's so bad about the "hired hand" (verses 12–13)?

Okay. So what's the result when anyone but the shepherd cares for the sheep?

Who is the Good Shepherd? How is his care for the sheep different from what anyone else offers (verses 11, 15, 17)?

BIG QUESTIONS The second half of verse 10 is an incredibly famous verse. What does it say about why Jesus showed up on planet earth?

INSIGHT Go back and reread about the shepherd's voice in verses 3–5. A shepherd didn't *drive* sheep from behind with a "yee-haw-git-along-little-doggies." He *led* them. The sheep recognized the shepherd's voice and unique call and were smart enough to follow the voice of their good guy—and scatter at the voice of a stranger. So what is Jesus saying about himself?

How have you seen God's kindness? What good things do you have because you belong to him?

What do you suppose his voice sounds like? What makes you want to follow him?

Put this all together—your pros and cons of being a Christian, what Jesus says about his kind and clear voice, and how he came to give you life. Do you believe all this stuff? Here are three true/false facts. Circle what you really think, not what you're supposed to answer:

T F Yep, I'm like a sheep; I need God's protection and care.
T F Yep, Jesus is a good shepherd.
T F Yep, if I were a sheep I'd sign up to have Jesus as my shepherd.

DEEP THOT It's hard to admit you're sheeplike, that you need protection and provision. But you'll never accept that care from Jesus unless you're convinced he's really the Good Shepherd who came to give you life.

STICKY STUFF Put John 10:10 in your sheep pen and don't let it scamper away.

ACT ON IT Inteview three mature Christians about why they decided to follow Jesus—and why they keep following.

DIG ON Check out Psalm 23 for great news on how God cares for you like a shepherd watches over his sheep.

5. Fly Away Home

God wants you home

Megan caught herself. As she tiptoed out the front door of her parents' house, she remembered her plan to leave the door unlocked and cracked open, knowing that if she pulled the door shut her parents would awaken. It wasn't until several days later that Megan had the sense to come home. Late at night she stood quietly at the front door. It was unlocked. Cracked open. And inside, her parents had left the lights on.

BRAIN DRAIN Have you ever felt like running away? Why or why not?

FLASHBACK You maybe know the story in this Bible Chunk. It's about two brothers and how they get along with their dad, and it's traditionally called the parable of "the prodigal son." But pay attention to the brothers and ask yourself how they're different—and how they're the same. This story looks long, but it snaps right along. Love, jealousy, pig slop—this tearjerker's got it all.

BIBLE CHUNK Read Luke 15:11–32

(11) Jesus continued: "There was a man who had two sons. (12) The younger one said to his father, 'Father, give me my share of the estate.' So he divided his property between them.

(13) "Not long after that, the younger son got together all he had, set off for a distant country and there squandered his wealth in wild living. (14) After he had spent everything, there was a severe famine in that whole country, and he began to be in need. (15) So he went and hired himself out to a citizen of that country, who sent him to his fields to feed pigs. (16) He

longed to fill his stomach with the pods that the pigs were eating, but no one gave him anything.

(17) "When he came to his senses, he said, 'How many of my father's hired men have food to spare, and here I am starving to death! (18) I will set out and go back to my father and say to him: Father, I have sinned against heaven and against you. (19) I am no longer worthy to be called your son; make me like one of your hired men.' (20) So he got up and went to his father.

"But while he was still a long way off, his father saw him and was filled with compassion for him; he ran to his son, threw his arms around him and kissed him.

(21) "The son said to him, 'Father, I have sinned against heaven and against you. I am no longer worthy to be called your son.'

(22) "But the father said to his servants, 'Quick! Bring the best robe and put it on him. Put a ring on his finger and sandals on his feet. (23) Bring the fattened calf and kill it. Let's have a feast and celebrate. (24) For this son of mine was dead and is alive again; he was lost and is found.' So they began to celebrate.

(25) "Meanwhile, the older son was in the field. When he came near the house, he heard music and dancing. (26) So he called one of the servants and asked him what was going on. (27) 'Your brother has come,' he replied, 'and your father has killed the fattened calf because he has him back safe and sound.'

(28) "The older brother became angry and refused to go in. So his father went out and pleaded with him. (29) But he answered his father, 'Look! All these years I've been slaving for you and never disobeyed your orders. Yet you never gave me even a young goat so I could celebrate with my friends. (30) But when this son of yours who has squandered your property with prostitutes comes home, you kill the fattened calf for him!'

(31) " 'My son,' the father said, 'you are always with me, and everything I have is yours. (32) But we had to celebrate and be glad, because this brother of yours was dead and is alive again; he was lost and is found.' "

INSIGHT The younger son wasn't hitting up his dad for next week's allowance—or even asking for help with the first hunk of money toward a house. His demand for an early inheritance was like screaming, "Dad, I wish you were dead!"

STUFF TO KNOW So exactly how are the older and younger brothers the same?

Puzzled? That might be the biggest point of the story. Here's a hint at how the wild young slob and the hyper-responsible firstborn son are the same: What's the older son doing when you first see him (verse 24)? What's his attitude as he serves his dad? (verses 29–30)

INSIGHT The older son was probably entitled to a double portion of the family wealth, and besides that he had nonstop access to the benefits of his father's house (verse 31). So while the younger son's trip to the pigpen was bad, just as sad is this fact: The older son is distant from his dad and doesn't know it.

DA'SCOOP Here's a great word to describe the sons' situation: "estranged." It means "hostile," "unsympathetic," "indifferent," and "alienated." That's how the sons are the same: They're both estranged from Dad.

BIG QUESTIONS Why didn't the father just ground the younger son?

That's partly a stupid question because the younger son was presumably grown-up. But here's the point: The father lets his son make a choice and roll in the stinky consequences. Likewise, God gives you a choice in how you relate to him.

How have you ditched God?

Have you ever stuck close to God and lived like he wants—but had an awful attitude? How?

Last one. Think about how you'd fit into the story and circle your pick:

a. I'm like the younger brother at the start of the story—I live a long way from God.
b. I'm like the older brother—I'm a Christian because I have to be.
c. I'm like the younger brother at the end. I know that God loves me no matter what and I want to stick close to him.
d. I don't have an answer right now.

DEEP THOT As much as God loves us, all of us are in some way at some time estranged from God—hostile, unsympathetic, indifferent, and alienated. But more than anything, God wants us home.

STICKY STUFF In a story connected to the Bible Chunk you read, Jesus told how a shepherd searched for his lost sheep just like the father in this story welcomes home his wandering son. Memorize this verse: "There is more rejoicing in heaven over one sinner who repents than over ninety-nine righteous persons who do not need to repent" (Luke 15:7). Lest you think you should run amok to make God smile, remember that all of us are *already* sinners. Those "righteous persons" just think they don't need to admit they are wrong.

ACT ON IT Roll in some pig slop or pick up after a pet to remind yourself what life is like when you live far from Jesus.

DIG ON Read Luke 15:1–15 to find out about the shepherd who looks for his lost sheep.

Talk About It • 1

EMPATHIZE: What's going on in your life?
ENCOURAGE: How are you doing with Jesus?
EQUIP: What one truth will you take home today?

- How do you react when people try to tell you about God? (Study 1)
- If Jesus knocked on your head and heart and said, "I want to get to know you and I want you to know me," how would you respond? (Study 1)
- What's it mean that Jesus is the "true bread"? (Study 2)
- So what attracts you to Jesus? What scares you away from following him? (Study 2)
- What do you think about the fact that God knows you absolutely up-close-and-personal? (Study 3)
- What's good and bad about being a Christian—what are the pros and cons? (Study 4)
- Where do you fit in the Bible's story of the runaway son?
  a. I'm like the younger brother at the start of the story—I live a long way from God.
  b. I'm like the older brother—I'm a Christian because I have to be.
  c. I'm like the younger brother at the end. I know that God loves me no matter what and I want to stick close to him.
  d. I don't have an answer right now.

PART 2

GRABBING HOLD OF GOD

6. The Rip in the Curtain

You can approach God boldly

Your mug shot and fingerprints probably don't decorate the post office. You've never been featured on *America's Most Wanted.* And you've never caused the face of anyone's pet hamster to appear on the back of a milk carton. So maybe you think you qualify to hang out with God.

Think again. Hard-to-Face Factoid #1: All of us have sinned—done wrong to God and others (Romans 3:23). Hard-to-Face Factoid #2: Just like what happens with any other friend we use or abuse, sin builds a wall between us and God. The Bible says, "You are not a God who takes pleasure in evil; with you the wicked cannot dwell" (Psalm 5:4). Hard-to-Face Factoid #3: God's punishment for sin is death—total, permanent separation from God and everything good (Romans 6:23).

BRAIN DRAIN What happens to your friendship when you nastily wrong a friend—or someone wrongs you?

FLASHBACK This Bible Chunk refers back to that Old Testament practice of sacrifice—that 3-D picture of the price of evil. Christ's death was a once-for-all sacrifice that put an end to that system (Hebrews 10:10–11). This Bible Chunk is one of the coolest you'll ever find, but it's got a lot to digest. Give it a quick read and catch the explanation below.

BIBLE CHUNK Hebrews 10:19–23

(19) Therefore, brothers, since we have confidence to enter the Most Holy Place by the blood of Jesus, (20) by a new and living way opened for

us through the curtain, that is, his body, (21) and since we have a great priest over the house of God, (22) let us draw near to God with a sincere heart in full assurance of faith, having our hearts sprinkled to cleanse us from a guilty conscience and having our bodies washed with pure water. (23) Let us hold unswervingly to the hope we profess, for he who promised is faithful.

INSIGHT Ever since Adam and Eve and the apple back at the very start of the Bible (Genesis 3), sin has built a wall between God and people. Before Christ, people got close to God chiefly at the temple in Jerusalem, and the temple's "Most Holy Place" was as close as anyone could get. Only once a year did God allow the high priest to slip through a curtain into this special place of his presence. The priest's position didn't get him in. Neither did nicey-nice sweet talk. His entrance pass was blood, and if anyone dared enter in a way other than what God prescribed, God nailed him dead.

That's a staggering image of the badness of bad and the awesomeness of God's perfection. Knowing all that, read your Bible Chunk again and see if it makes more sense.

STUFF TO KNOW Now that you've got a grasp on that big idea, why would having "the blood of Jesus" make you confident to enter God's presence?

Baffled? Here's an explanation: The "blood of Jesus" isn't a magic potion like toenail clippings and bat's breath that forces God to accept you. It's the death Jesus died on the cross.

SIDELIGHT Sinning against God isn't just dissing a friend, it's disrespecting the God of the Universe. It's an infinite crime with an infinite penalty. Hundreds of years before Jesus, the Bible predicted a savior would take the punishment people deserve for the wrong we do. He would die in our place for what the Bible calls "sin," "transgression," or "iniquity":

But he was pierced for our transgressions, he was crushed for our iniquities; the punishment that brought us peace was upon him,

> and by his wounds we are healed. We all, like sheep, have gone astray, each of us has turned to his own way; and the Lord has laid on him the iniquity of us all. (Isaiah 53:5–6)

Who took the punishment you deserve?

So how can you approach God now (verse 22)?

While having your "heart sprinkled" and "body washed" sounds like a visit to a scrub-o-matic Laundromat, it actually refers to the cleansing that takes place when God makes you his friend. You stand spanking clean before God. Your sins are washed away. That's why you can swap fear for boldness.

SIDELIGHT When Jesus died on the cross, the sky turned black and the earth shook. But another thing happened: That curtain blocking the way to the Most Holy Place tore in two (Matthew 27:51). God forever ripped open a way to himself no one can sew shut.

BIG QUESTIONS Tell in your own words how Christ's death makes you acceptable to God. What has Christ done for you?

This next question sounds like the setup for a bad joke, but what would you say if you died and arrived at the gates of heaven and God said, "Why should I let you in?"

If you don't have an answer ready for that right now, keep mulling that question. But have you ever thought to yourself, *I believe this stuff. I believe that Jesus died for the wrong things I've done?*

What keeps people from admitting to God—or even to themselves—that they've done wrong?

DEEP THOT God's love is unfathomable and unchangeable. But God can't live with sin. Jesus came to do something about that—something that shows that evil won't go unpunished *and* that allows you to get back to God. That's what he did for you when he died on the cross.

STICKY STUFF Focus Hebrews 10:22 in the front of your mind and you'll keep a bold confidence in your friendship with God. As always, there's a card in the back.

ACT ON IT Beg three people to tell you how they think they can get God to like them. What's the real way you're accepted by God?

DIG ON Check out these key verses for understanding how Christ died in our place: Romans 3:21–26 and Romans 6:23. Or dig into Leviticus 16 to get a picture of what sacrifice meant before Christ became the final sacrifice.

7. Deep Thots

How God makes you his friend

Jared flipped campfire coals with the end of a stick. He stared at the fire, trying to figure out his friends. His camp mates were suddenly spiritual, bawling about how bad they were and how good God was. Part of him thought it was cool they could be honest. Another part thought all that sobbing was a show. *I don't want anything fake,* he finally decided. *If I'm going to get God, I want what's real. I want to be sure about my faith.*

BRAIN DRAIN What would it mean to you to know—for sure—that you are God's friend? How much does it matter to you?

FLASHBACK Colossians came from the pen of one of the early church's major leaders to convince readers of the greatness of Jesus—of who he is and all he does. The apostle Paul says Christ is the "image of the invisible God" and that all the "fullness" of God dwells in him. Get this: Jesus isn't a fuzzy photocopy of God. He's one of a kind. He's God the Son, fully God and fully human. Along with God the Father and God the Holy Spirit, Jesus is a member of the Trinity—the "one-being-three-person" entity we call God. While it may bend your brain to ponder that, the Bible will make more sense if you do.

BIBLE CHUNK Read Colossians 1:15–23

(15) He [Christ] is the image of the invisible God, the firstborn over all creation. (16) For by him all things were created: things in heaven and on

earth, visible and invisible, whether thrones or powers or rulers or authorities; all things were created by him and for him. (17) He is before all things, and in him all things hold together. (18) And he is the head of the body, the church; he is the beginning and the firstborn from among the dead, so that in everything he might have the supremacy. (19) For God was pleased to have all his fullness dwell in him, (20) and through him to reconcile to himself all things, whether things on earth or things in heaven, by making peace through his blood, shed on the cross.

(21) Once you were alienated from God and were enemies in your minds because of your evil behavior. (22) But now he has reconciled you by Christ's physical body through death to present you holy in his sight, without blemish and free from accusation—(23) if you continue in your faith, established and firm, not moved from the hope held out in the gospel. This is the gospel that you heard and that has been proclaimed to every creature under heaven, and of which I, Paul, have become a servant.

STUFF TO KNOW You might be smart about the details of the life, death, and resurrection of Jesus, but you probably don't think of him as the maker of this world. But what all did he make (verse 16)?

Not only was everything made "by" Jesus but "for" Jesus. It's like going to art class and making a clay pot: You make it, you da master of it. Now, here's another way to look at what you read in the last lesson. What all did Christ do for you (verses 20, 22)?

DA'SCOOP You might be hazy on what "reconcile" precisely means. It's to "reestablish a close relationship." It comes from the word "conciliate," which means "to overcome distrust" or "to regain good will." Jesus' death is what reconciles us to God.

Why did you need reconciling—what are people like before they know God (verse 21)?

If you're like every other human on earth, you start out as an enemy of God with bad thoughts and bad behavior. What does God think of you once you have been reconciled through Christ's death (verse 22)?

One last one. "Gospel" means "good news." What does Paul say is the "Good News" that you and every other creature crawling the earth has heard (verse 23)?

SIDELIGHT You may have memorized the ultrafamous Bible verse John 3:16: "For God so loved the world that he gave his one and only Son, that whoever believes in him shall not perish but have eternal life." What you're reading in this and other Bible Chunks are sort of expanded ways to say how God "gave his only Son."

BIG QUESTIONS Do you feel like God's friend? What makes you sure—or not sure?

Go back and underline verses 21–23. How does the Bible say you can change from being God's enemy to being God's friend?

Those three verses sum up how you get straight with God. They're great for getting a grip on what Jesus has done for you. Take a look at them in the easy-to-read *New Century Version* of the Bible:

- You—and all people—have a PROBLEM (verse 21): "At one time you were separated from God. You were enemies in your minds, and the evil things you did were against God."

- God has a SOLUTION (verse 22): "But now God has made you his friends again. He did this through Christ's death in the body so that he might bring you into God's presence as people who are holy, with no wrong, and with nothing of which God can judge you guilty."
- And there's a right RESPONSE (verse 23) to make to God's SOLUTION to your PROBLEM: "This will happen if you continue strong and sure in your faith. You must not be moved away from the hope brought to you by the Good News that you heard."

Belief in this "Good News" isn't just "Yeah, I agree with that in my head." Having "faith" (verse 23) means you can say, "I trust my life to that." Huge question: Have you responded to God's solution to your problem with that kind of faith? How?

DEEP THOT Maybe you grew up trusting that Jesus died for your sins. Or maybe you've never grabbed hold of God's Good News. God knows what's in your heart, but it's good for *you* to know he knows. You can tell God something like this: "God, I know I've wronged you. I trust that Jesus died for my sins. Thank you for making me your friend, and help me stick close to you." When you begin to believe in Jesus—to accept who he is and what he has done for you—you change from being God's enemy to being God's friend.

STICKY STUFF Colossians 1:21–22 is the core of your faith, so pop it in your cerebrum and cork it so it doesn't ooze out.

ACT ON IT Tell a friend how you've responded to God's solution to your problem.

DIG ON Check out Colossians 1:13–14 and 2:23 for two more ways to describe what it means to become God's friends.

8. Chicken Dance

God promises to forgive you

You press Load on your friend's parents' ultra-expensive CD deck, expecting to hear your beloved "Chicken Dance." Instead, a wisp of smoke emerges and wafts up your nostrils. You didn't try to make the stereo die, but it did. You quietly exit the party at your first chance, and now you're scared to ever step foot again in your friend's house. Your friend never talks about it. You don't know if the parents know you did it. And you're not about to knock on their door and say, "Oh, I'm the one who jammed your CD player with disk 5 of my *101 Polka Party Favorites Collection*. But you wish you had a way to get everything out in the open—to bring truth to light.

BRAIN DRAIN What's it like to be home alone when the power—and all the lights—go out? What can't you do in the darkness?

FLASHBACK This Bible Chunk starts almost at the beginning of 1 John, a short letter written by the same disciple of Jesus who wrote the long Bible book of John. He starts this brief note by saying that Jesus is a real guy he saw and knew—and that he came to bring us life.

BIBLE CHUNK Read 1 John 1:5–2:6. If you have a hard time following this passage, go ahead and scribble in some simpler words. Where it says "walk," think "live." Where it says "fellowship," think "closeness." And where it says "confess our sins," think "admit our sins to God."

> (1:5) This is the message we have heard from him and declare to you: God is light; in him there is no darkness at all. (1:6) If we claim to have fellow-

ship with him yet walk in the darkness, we lie and do not live by the truth. (1:7) But if we walk in the light, as he is in the light, we have fellowship with one another, and the blood of Jesus, his Son, purifies us from all sin.

(1:8) If we claim to be without sin, we deceive ourselves and the truth is not in us. (1:9) If we confess our sins, he is faithful and just and will forgive us our sins and purify us from all unrighteousness. (1:10) If we claim we have not sinned, we make him out to be a liar and his word has no place in our lives. (2:1) My dear children, I write this to you so that you will not sin. But if anybody does sin, we have one who speaks to the Father in our defense—Jesus Christ, the Righteous One. (2:2) He is the atoning sacrifice for our sins, and not only for ours but also for the sins of the whole world.

(2:3) We know that we have come to know him if we obey his commands. (2:4) The man who says, "I know him," but does not do what he commands is a liar, and the truth is not in him. (2:5) But if anyone obeys his word, God's love is truly made complete in him. This is how we know we are in him: (2:6) Whoever claims to live in him must walk as Jesus did.

STUFF TO KNOW What is God, according to verse 1:5?

"Light" stands for a bunch of things, but especially purity and truth. So what happens when you walk in the dark (verse 1:6)?

INSIGHT Not that long ago you probably freaked in the night. Monsters lurked in closets and boogeypersons cast shadows on your bedroom wall. That's the kind of scary darkness John means—the pitch black of a moonless, cloudy night with no streetlights, shopping malls, or twenty-four-hour gas stations in sight. Wander off and you're lost, just like when you wander out of God's light you're *spiritually* lost.

Walking in God's light is a choice you make. What happens once you're in the light (verse 1:7)?

INSIGHT Even if the dark sounds bad, strutting into God's light sounds scary too—more of those I'm-not-sure-I-like-that-God-knows-everything-about-me fears. It's scary, that is, until you realize why God shines his light to reveal everything for what it truly is. God can already see everything. Light is for *you* to see who and where you are. God's goal is to help you, not hurt you.

How does walking in the light happen (verses 1:8–9)?

One last one—and it can't get any more obvious than this. Why is John writing (verse 2:1)?

SIDELIGHT When you become a Christian, God starts changing and growing you and promises not to stop until you're like him (Philippians 1:6). You don't become immediately perfect. This side of heaven, in fact, you won't become totally unflawed. You're kidding yourself to think anything else. (In case you doubt that, here's a test. Ask your mother if you ever mess up. Ask your friends about your ugly side. Or flip through the Bible to find yourself in one of these lists: Ephesians 4:25–5:4 or Galatians 5:19–21.)

BIG QUESTIONS So you're a Christian. And you just did something wrong. God's got two options. When you've fallen down he could wag a finger at you and then whack you. But he'd like to help you up. So what does God want *you* to do (verse 1:9)?

Then what does the Bible promise he will do (verse 1:9)?

But what's the danger in God saying "My forgiveness is always available to you?"

INSIGHT The point of 1 John 2:1–6 is that if you continue to sin, you maybe haven't understood the walloping greatness of God's kind forgiveness. Or maybe you don't know that God wants not only to forgive you but to change you. If you find yourself trapped over and over by sin, ask God to help you figure out what's up inside you. And remember that he makes an unbreakable promise: Jesus is the sacrifice that paid for your sins.

DEEP THOT Admitting your sin is how you get everything into the light, grab hold of God's forgiveness, and get on with your relationship. Real Christians aren't people who never mess up; they're the ones who get up and go on. So keep two facts in your head: *Fact 1:* Even as a Christian you sin, and sin strains your relationships with God and people. *Fact 2:* But you have God's promise: If you confess wrongs, God forgives.

ACT ON IT Some Christians who mess up can't accept God's forgiveness when they fess up. If that's you, find a wise older Christian to talk to.

STICKY STUFF It's a sure thing you'll need this verse tomorrow—if not today: 1 John 1:8–9.

DIG ON Read what John wrote earlier in his life about Jesus being the light in John 3:17–21. It's got a lot to say about God shining his light to help you, not hurt you.

9. You Are What You Schedule

The greatness of knowing Jesus

Dig into your Day-Timer, your Palm Pilot or PocketPC, your assignment planner, the left half of your head, or wherever else you organize your life. What ranks high on your list of hot stuff to do? Imagine pouring all that stuff in a test tube and torching it over a Bunsen burner like a science class mystery liquid. What do you get when you boil it to the last drop? What's your life made of?

BRAIN DRAIN If you asked a dozen people to identify the most important thing in your life, what would they say? What evidence would they offer?

FLASHBACK The apostle Paul was about as religious a person as you could find. Right before this Bible Chunk, he reeled off all the ways he had his life straight. In this passage he says that *all* the important stuff about him is garbage. Is he weird or what?

BIBLE CHUNK Read Philippians 3:7–11

> (7) But whatever was to my profit I [Paul] now consider loss for the sake of Christ. (8) What is more, I consider everything a loss compared to the surpassing greatness of knowing Christ Jesus my Lord, for whose sake I have lost all things. I consider them rubbish, that I may gain Christ (9) and be found in him, not having a righteousness of my own that comes from the law, but that which is through faith in Christ—the righteousness that comes from God and is by faith. (10) I want to know Christ and the power of his resurrection and the fellowship of sharing in his sufferings, becom-

ing like him in his death, (11) and so, somehow, to attain to the resurrection from the dead.

STUFF TO KNOW Rewind: Remember that Paul is saying all these things are worthless. (7) What do you think he means by that?

INSIGHT Paul's got a double meaning here. Point 1: All the things he thought mattered are "loss for the sake of Christ" because he had used them to earn God's approval. The only thing Paul wants now is to be approved by God based on what Christ did on the cross. Point 2: Those good things actually got in the way of his knowing Christ. He's putting them away—to the point that he calls them garbage. The word he uses means "worthless trash" or, to be more vivid, "dung." Compared with knowing Christ, everything else is like sqwooshing a cow pie.

So what's the most important thing in the world to Paul (verse 8)?

And how is Paul going to be accepted by God (verse 9)?

Paul doesn't want to earn God's approval by keeping "the law"—God's commands. As important as it is to obey God, he can only get right with God by faith in Christ.

DA'SCOOP Time to learn some big words that keep popping up in the Bible Chunks you're reading. Start with "reconciliation," one you already know. It's making friends again. "Forgiveness" is God wiping clean your sins and not holding them against you. "Justification" is a legal term that means God declaring you "not guilty." "Righteousness" can mean either goodness or right standing before God. "Grace" is the fact that everything God gives you is a free gift, especially his favor. "Faith" is your belief and trust in God and his promises. And "salvation" is the whole package of what God does for you, saving you from the penalty, power, and—in heaven—the presence of sin.

What does Paul say it means to know Christ? Look for four things in verses 10 and 11.

SIDELIGHT Paul talks about knowing Christ in deep ways: the power of Christ's resurrection (to experience God's life-changing strength), the fellowship of Christ's sufferings (living and giving like Jesus, even when it hurts), being like Christ in death (ditching stuff that gets in the way of God's plans), and attaining to the resurrection from the dead (living in heaven forever with God).

SIDELIGHT You have nothing to show off to score points with God, because nothing you can do can earn more of his love. Ephesians 2:8–9 says, "For it is by grace you have been saved, through faith—and this not from yourselves, it is the gift of God—not by works, so that no one can boast." Your friendship with God is a total gift.

BIG QUESTIONS What good things about you do you think make you matter—to God and other people?

Even if you don't strut your good stuff to impress God, it can get in the way of your friendship if it makes you too busy, too absorbed, or too tired to spend time and energy getting to know God. Is it Jesus-freaky weirdly spiritual to think that good, normal, everyday stuff can crowd out God? Why or who not? Be honest.

But even so, do you have any of that good, normal, everyday stuff going on that crowds out God? Details, please.

How does your schedule show what place God has in your life? Is he first on your list, last on your list, or not on your list at all?

What one change could you make to your life to put Christ first?

How is what you read in verses 10 and 11 like—or not like—your friendship with Jesus?

DEEP THOT Paul's point is short and sweet: He can't think of anything better than being best friends with Christ. He wouldn't wish anything less for you.

STICKY STUFF Philippians 3:8 will help you keep first things first. Use it to test your time-management tactics.

ACT ON IT Rummage through your calendar and find time you can spend on radically important spiritual stuff.

DIG ON Read Psalm 63 to catch a bit of what it means to really want to know God.

10. Inside Out

Why you live for God

Peers might make fun of you for going to church. They might un-invite you to parties for following Jesus and making them feel guilty about their "fun." They might pass you at school and scurry away like you just passed—well, something stinky. But if you've got God, you've got something real you can't deny. And no one has to force you to live for him.

BRAIN DRAIN What makes Jesus worth following because you want to—not because you have to?

FLASHBACK Last time you read in Philippians how ultra-important it is to know God. In the Bible book of 2 Corinthians Paul unleashes even more reasons for being a follower of Christ. The readers he had poured himself into now sass and insult him because they think they're more spiritual than him and that his sacrificial dedication to God is a little dense. "You think I'm crazy? You want to know why I'm so nuts about God?" he asks. "I'll tell you."

BIBLE CHUNK Read 2 Corinthians 5:14–21

(14) For Christ's love compels us, because we are convinced that one died for all, and therefore all died. (15) And he died for all, that those who live should no longer live for themselves but for him who died for them and was raised again. (16) So from now on we regard no one from a worldly point of view. Though we once regarded Christ in this way, we do so no longer. (17) Therefore, if anyone is in Christ, he is a new creation; the old has gone, the new has come! (18) All this is from God, who reconciled us to himself through Christ and gave us the ministry of reconcil-

iation: (19) that God was reconciling the world to himself in Christ, not counting men's sins against them. And he has committed to us the message of reconciliation. (20) We are therefore Christ's ambassadors, as though God were making his appeal through us. We implore you on Christ's behalf: Be reconciled to God. (21) God made him who had no sin to be sin for us, so that in him we might become the righteousness of God.

STUFF TO KNOW Okay. Remember the topic of discussion was "You want to know why I'm so crazy?" Given that, why is Paul so nuts about being a Christian (verses 14–15)?

INSIGHT It's like this. Take a man and a woman deeply in love. Not just smoochy-smoochy love, but bonded in their emotions and committed with their wills. You don't have to force them to care for each other. They love because they want to, not because they have to. That's the kind of live-for-God passion that drives Christians. God gave himself for you, dying in your place. Now you can give yourself back to him by obeying him.

A real change takes place when you become a Christian, when you are "in Christ." What is it (verse 17)?

What's the old stuff that's gone? Peek at verses 19 and 21 for hints. What happens, for starters, to your sin and guilt?

Think hard: What is the new stuff that starts when someone decides to get God?

INSIGHT That's difficult to get from this Bible Chunk alone.

But a new life has started that is as clear as a brand-new baby popping from the womb. To see a believer as anything less than that new creature is "worldly" or unspiritual.

Who is the cause of this "new you" (verse 18)?

And what's the result of God acting in your life? What further responsibility and privilege does God bequeath to you (verses 18–20)?

BIG QUESTIONS You might wonder if Paul is dealing in reality when he says you're "new." If you've done drugs, you likely won't immediately and completely stop struggling with temptations to abuse chemicals because you've become a Christian. If you've pushed past God's limits with a boyfriend or girlfriend, you'll have to break that relationship before you'll be able to break that habit. The battle between good and evil rages on inside you even after you become a Christian (check out Romans 7 and Galatians 5). But here's Paul's point: If you've become a Christian, then underneath it all you've been reborn.

So what motivates you to follow God? Do you live as a Christian because you want to—or because something makes you feel you have to?

What about you is different from what it would be if you weren't a Christian?

Are you powered to follow God by something that keeps going and going—or does your desire to live for God start, sputter, and stop?

INSIGHT Real change comes from the inside out. It starts with your new relationship with God. That affects your attitudes. It moves out into your actions. And then it splashes out on other people.

So who do you know who could use a splash of God's love? Who do you know who doesn't know God—who still lives as God's enemy?

What can you do to show that person God and to share that "message of reconciliation"?

Talking about your faith can get tricky—and scary. But wouldn't you like the world to have what you have? Why or why not?

DEEP THOT This is gigantic stuff. Your Christian faith won't last if it's founded on fear. It won't be fun at all if the only motivation you can muster is terror that God wants to trash you. It's only a blast when God's love rules your life, when you can say, "God loves me and I'm gonna love him back."

STICKY STUFF Jam this one in your brain juice: 2 Corinthians 5:14–15.

ACT ON IT Pray for a friend who needs to hear God's cool "message of reconciliation."

DIG ON Your friendship with God isn't just for today. It's for eternity. Read Revelation 22 to find out what God has planned for you.

Talk About It • 2

EMPATHIZE: What's going on in your life?
ENCOURAGE: How are you doing with Jesus?
EQUIP: What one truth will you take home today?

- Do you feel like God's friend? What makes you sure—or not sure? (Study 7)
- Tell in your own words how Christ's death makes you acceptable to God. How does "the blood of Jesus" make you confident to enter God's presence? (Study 6)
- Or how does the Bible say you can change from being God's enemy to being God's friend? (Study 7)
- You're a Christian. You just did something wrong. Is God going to wag a finger at you and whack you? How would he like to help you up? What's 1 John 1:8–9 say? (Study 8)
- How can you tell if God is the most important thing in your life? (Study 9)
- What one change could you make in your life to put Christ first? (Study 9)
- Can you expect instant changes when you become a Christian? What changes? What doesn't? (Study 9)
- What powers you to follow God? Is it something that keeps going—or does your desire to live for God start, sputter, and stop? (Study 10)
- What's 2 Corinthians 5:14–15 say about what can motivate you to follow Jesus? (Study 10)

PART 3

FIGURING OUT GOD'S FAITHFULNESS

11. Where's the Bathroom?

God's care for you

Jessica's parents panicked when she wanted to sign up for a year-long student exchange program to a country where she didn't know a word of the language. But they calmed when they heard she'd have someone looking out for her. The director of the exchange program happened to be the most powerful person in the country apart from the president. Even though Jessica couldn't say "Where's the bathroom?" she knew how to pronounce her protector's name. Say the name, she'd be safe.

BRAIN DRAIN Who's high on your helpful list? Where do you run when you're in trouble? And who do you trust to save you at any time, in any place, from any hazard?

FLASHBACK Just before this Bible Chunk God asked, "To whom will you compare me?" That's a question he'll ask again halfway through this passage. And along the way he'll point out wrong places you might put your trust.

BIBLE CHUNK Read Isaiah 40:21–31. "Jacob" and "Israel" in verse 27 are two names for God's Old Testament people, the Israelites, and the "he" at the beginning of verse 22 is God. Write that in big.

> (21) Do you not know? Have you not heard? Has it not been told you from the beginning? Have you not understood since the earth was founded? (22) He sits enthroned above the circle of the earth, and its people are like grasshoppers. He stretches out the heavens like a canopy, and

spreads them out like a tent to live in. (23) He brings princes to naught and reduces the rulers of this world to nothing. (24) No sooner are they planted, no sooner are they sown, no sooner do they take root in the ground, than he blows on them and they wither, and a whirlwind sweeps them away like chaff.

(25) "To whom will you compare me? Or who is my equal?" says the Holy One. (26) Lift your eyes and look to the heavens: Who created all these? He who brings out the starry host one by one, and calls them each by name. Because of his great power and mighty strength, not one of them is missing.

(27) Why do you say, O Jacob, and complain, O Israel, "My way is hidden from the Lord; my cause is disregarded by my God"? (28) Do you not know? Have you not heard? The Lord is the everlasting God, the Creator of the ends of the earth. He will not grow tired or weary, and his understanding no one can fathom. (29) He gives strength to the weary and increases the power of the weak. (30) Even youths grow tired and weary, and young men stumble and fall; (31) but those who hope in the Lord will renew their strength. They will soar on wings like eagles; they will run and not grow weary, they will walk and not be faint.

STUFF TO KNOW

God is an infinity higher than anyone or anything else you might trust your life to—any other god, person, or thing you might think is ultimately powerful. Take a look at the whole Bible Chunk you read and list ways God is big, bold, and better.

Explain how famous, influential people measure up to God (verses 23–24).

How big are the rest of us normal people next to God (verse 22)?

What is God like size-wise compared to the most immense stuff you can spot with the Hubble telescope—sky and space (verses 22, 26)?

And how is God unlike everything that gets tired, wears down, or goes stupid (verse 28)?

God does some righteous stuff with that incomparable power. How does he use his might (verses 29–31)?

BIG QUESTIONS How would you handle being as all-powerful and all-knowing as God? Would you run around like a four-year-old on a hot summer day stomping every ant in sight? In thirty words or less, write "If I were King of the Universe I would . . ."

God puts good, wise, even powerful people in your life to help you. What people take care of you when you're needy or tired?

Even though you've got people on your side, what can God provide that people can't?

What does God promise you if you trust him?

SIDELIGHT You can pry open your eyes to God's care with these bright words of Jesus in Matthew 11:28–30: "Come to me, all you who are weary and burdened, and I will give you rest. Take my yoke upon you and learn from me, for I am gentle and humble in heart, and you will find rest for your souls."

How is this picture of God different from what loads of people think about him?

DEEP THOT Roll together all of God's qualities—all-powerful, all-loving, totally just, completely caring. You couldn't invent a better helper or a bigger God.

STICKY STUFF Put Isaiah 40:31 in your mind for your next miserable day.

ACT ON IT Draw a picture, write a song, or compose a poem of what God's care for you looks like.

DIG ON Read Psalm 46 for more on God's care when your world collapses.

12. Battle Droids

God understands your weakness

Despite hours in front of a mirror, you've never actually spotted a tiny cartoon devil sitting on one of your shoulders and a tiny angel on the other. Yet you know they're there—or at least you feel like they are. Every time you're tempted to do wrong they bat your brain back and forth like a Ping-Pong ball. Ping: "Do evil!" Pong: "Do right!" Ping: "Do what *you* want!" Pong: "Do what *God* wants!" You'd like to whack them both.

BRAIN DRAIN What's the worst situation you've ever been in where you were tempted to do wrong—but didn't? What got you through?

FLASHBACK A few pages back you learned that Jesus is the great high priest who paved the path for you back to God. This next Bible Chunk actually shows up several Bible chapters before what you read from Hebrews 10. It's short but sweet.

BIBLE CHUNK Read Hebrews 4:14–16

> (14) Therefore, since we have a great high priest who has gone through the heavens, Jesus the Son of God, let us hold firmly to the faith we profess. (15) For we do not have a high priest who is unable to sympathize with our weaknesses, but we have one who has been tempted in every way, just as we are—yet was without sin. (16) Let us then approach the throne of grace with confidence, so that we may receive mercy and find grace to help us in our time of need.

STUFF TO KNOW What's it matter that Jesus felt tempted to do wrong (verse 15)?

INSIGHT God possesses total knowledge, so he's always understood temptation. But this Bible Chunk makes you extra-aware that he comprehends what temptation looks like, tastes like, smells like, and feels like. Jesus' coming to earth as a human being—God in a bod—means *you* know he knows.

DA'SCOOP The meaning of "great high priest" here isn't only that Jesus offered his life on your behalf but that he now reigns in heaven. The term might be hard to grasp because it's from an ancient time and culture, but this passage says that what Jesus does as great high priest is reason to hang tight to your faith.

How did Jesus react to temptation (verse 15)?

How does knowing that Jesus understands temptation help you when you feel tempted (verse 16)?

BIG QUESTIONS Have you ever pondered the fact that Christ was genuinely tempted to do wrong just like you? What do you think: Is that bizarre or what?

What are the biggest temptations you face?

Hey—be honest. What's the difference between your reaction to temptation and Jesus' reaction?

How do you battle temptation—or don't you?

SIDELIGHT When Jesus felt pulled to do wrong, he found two ways to get help. First, he prayed and dumped all his dreams and desires on God. When Jesus faced death on the cross, he was able to say, "Father, I don't want to go there. But I do want what you want" (Luke 22:42). Second, Jesus battled temptation with a God-given weapon. Spot how he fought back in Matthew 4:3–11:

> The tempter [the Devil] came to him and said, "If you are the Son of God, tell these stones to become bread." Jesus answered, "It is written: 'Man does not live on bread alone, but on every word that comes from the mouth of God.' " Then the devil took him to the holy city and had him stand on the highest point of the temple. "If you are the Son of God," he said, "throw yourself down. For it is written: " 'He will command his angels concerning you, and they will lift you up in their hands, so that you will not strike your foot against a stone.' " Jesus answered him, "It is also written: 'Do not put the Lord your God to the test.' " Again, the devil took him to a very high mountain and showed him all the kingdoms of the world and their splendor. "All this I will give you," he said, "if you will bow down and worship me." Jesus said to him, "Away from me, Satan! For it is written: 'Worship the Lord your God, and serve him only.' " Then the devil left him, and angels came and attended him.

Chances are you haven't had Satan himself pester you with trinkets like total control of the world. But from what you see in that Bible Chunk in Matthew, what does evil-fighting help look like? How does Jesus battle back?

INSIGHT You have access to the same weapon Jesus used:

truth. Sure, God *could* send an army of angels to your rescue, but he's already outfitted you with a temptation blaster—the facts of life found in the Bible.

What can you do the next time you feel tempted? Got any new ideas?

DEEP THOT The privilege of running to God doesn't do squat if you don't think he comprehends your need. But you have access to a powerful, no-one-beats-him God who understands perfectly the world of temptations you face.

STICKY STUFF Glue Hebrews 4:15–16 into your brain goo.

ACT ON IT Visit *www.thewave.org/GetGod.htm* for a downloadable rap version of Hebrews 4:15–16. The music makes the verse much stickier.

DIG ON Think of an area where you face frequent temptation. Use a concordance, Bible study software, topical Bible, or another Christian's wisdom to find verses that fit you to fight.

13. Ode to Eutychus

Why you need other Christians

The pastor drones into the megaphone with the same undeviating monotone that put you to sleep in the first place. "This is not a drill," he says. "I repeat, this is not a drill. We have a youth snoozing in the second row." He calls the ushers and elders forward to "revive this dear child." The way he says the word "re-vi-vah" reverbs through the church as elders quote Acts 20:9–10 at you—the story of a kid who nodded off in church, flopped out a third story-window, and died. Not that you were awake to hear any of this. . . .

BRAIN DRAIN What's beneficial—or bad or boring—about hanging out with other Christians at church, school, or wherever?

FLASHBACK You've already read what comes right before this Bible Chunk—that Hebrews 10 passage about how Christ has opened a new and living way to God. This next Bible Chunk is so short you'll miss it if you blink.

BIBLE CHUNK Read Hebrews 10:24–25

> (24) And let us consider how we may spur one another on toward love and good deeds. (25) Let us not give up meeting together, as some are in the habit of doing, but let us encourage one another—and all the more as you see the Day approaching.

STUFF TO KNOW The author of Hebrews just explained to his readers their fantastic new friendship with God through Christ. How does he tell them to keep it fresh (verse 24)?

What goal should you have for your relationships with one another (verse 24)?

SIDELIGHT The Bible pictures Christians as so interdependent that they're a body. Each part is unique. Each part is necessary. Read about it in 1 Corinthians 12.

What are you supposed to *not* stop doing (verse 25)?

Why (verse 24–25)?

INSIGHT "The Day approaching" is the return of Christ to planet earth. Elsewhere the Bible says Christians "ought to live holy and godly lives as you look forward to the day of God" (2 Peter 3:11–12). The point here is that you can't get ready for the return of Jesus all by your lonesome. You need to hang with the herd of fellow followers of Jesus.

BIG QUESTIONS Count on your fingers and toes if you need to, but figure out how often you get to church or other places where your main purpose is to grow with other Christians—like how many times have you been with believers in the past month?

What keeps you coming back—or what scares you away?

SIDELIGHT Christian friendship runs deeper than suffering silently together through a Sunday school lecture once a week. Hebrews 3:13 says to "encourage one another daily." Why? "So that none of you may be hardened by sin's deceitfulness." Truth is, you and your Christian friends are way more than roller coaster animals. You need time to socialize, but you also need spiritual stretching. Something is seriously wrong if your Christian relationships don't prod you closer to God.

Exactly how well does your church spur you on to do what's right? Plop a dot on the spectrum:

Total fun and games with no spiritual content .... Excessively serious with no chance to breathe

Pointed question: Is your church meeting your need to grow—and giving you a chance to boost others upward?

What goals do you have for getting together and grooving with Christian friends?

SIDELIGHT What you need from Christian sisters and brothers isn't a mystery. Here's a sneak peek at a verse you'll land on later in *Get God*: "Flee the evil desires of youth, and pursue righteousness, faith, love and peace, along with those who call on the Lord out of a pure heart" (2 Timothy 2:22). You need to hang out with people who hanker to obey Jesus.

Get practical. If you could invent a perfect Christian friend, what would she or he look like?

Well, that's nice. But it might not be realistic. After all, do *you* match that description? So how do you grow when the people around you are less than massively spiritually mature?

Which one or two Christian friends can you call when you need help? Prove it: What are their phone numbers or email addresses?

If you have a tough time making solid friends at church, what are you going to do about it? Who can you ask for help?

DEEP THOT The author of Hebrews wove a whole book around the theme that Jesus gives us incredible access to God. Right after he shouts, "Be bold in knowing God!" the very next thing he says is that you can't survive without Christian friends. The point: Don't stop at knowing God, but get to know his people too. An old Christian rock song said it straight: "If I just see you once a week, then why do we need each other?"

STICKY STUFF Memorize Hebrews 10:24–25. Better yet, memorize it with two friends.

ACT ON IT If you aren't involved in a church or youth group at least weekly, make a list of where to start—and get visiting.

DIG ON Even big believers in the Bible sometimes had a hard time finding the right friends. Read Elijah's moans in 1 Kings 19. Pay close attention to verses 14 and 19.

14. He's All You Need

God is with you even when you're lonely

Talia understood why her family had to move. But three months after she'd crated up all her worldly possessions, she felt picked on by every clique at her new school. She wanted to scream at the whole place that, yes, she had a whole *mob* of friends—but she couldn't prove it anyway, because they were back home at her old church. She couldn't decide which would be harder—to have had friends and left or to never have had friends at all. *Two more hours and Erica will be online to chat,* she thought. Talia shut her eyes and tried not to think till then.

BRAIN DRAIN Write about a time you felt incredibly ripped off by evil people—when they did dastardly evil and got no punishment.

FLASHBACK Bonus: You get a whole Bible chapter! Psalm 73 is worth an end-to-end read because it talks about one of life's most faith-squashing topics: why bad people succeed and good people feel ripped off. The author of the psalm, Asaph, was a master songwriter at the time of King David.

BIBLE CHUNK Read Psalm 73

(1) Surely God is good to Israel, to those who are pure in heart.

(2) But as for me, my feet had almost slipped; I had nearly lost my foothold. (3) For I envied the arrogant when I saw the prosperity of the wicked.

(4) They have no struggles; their bodies are healthy and strong. (5) They are free from the burdens common to man; they are not plagued by human ills. (6) Therefore pride is their necklace; they clothe themselves

with violence. (7) From their callous hearts comes iniquity; the evil conceits of their minds know no limits. (8) They scoff, and speak with malice; in their arrogance they threaten oppression. (9) Their mouths lay claim to heaven, and their tongues take possession of the earth. (10) Therefore their people turn to them and drink up waters in abundance. (11) They say, "How can God know? Does the Most High have knowledge?"

(12) This is what the wicked are like—always carefree, they increase in wealth.

(13) Surely in vain have I kept my heart pure; in vain have I washed my hands in innocence. (14) All day long I have been plagued; I have been punished every morning.

(15) If I had said, "I will speak thus," I would have betrayed your children. (16) When I tried to understand all this, it was oppressive to me (17) till I entered the sanctuary of God; then I understood their final destiny.

(18) Surely you place them on slippery ground; you cast them down to ruin. (19) How suddenly are they destroyed, completely swept away by terrors! (20) As a dream when one awakes, so when you arise, O Lord, you will despise them as fantasies.

(21) When my heart was grieved and my spirit embittered, (22) I was senseless and ignorant; I was a brute beast before you.

(23) Yet I am always with you; you hold me by my right hand. (24) You guide me with your counsel, and afterward you will take me into glory. (25) Whom have I in heaven but you? And earth has nothing I desire besides you. (26) My flesh and my heart may fail, but God is the strength of my heart and my portion forever.

(27) Those who are far from you will perish; you destroy all who are unfaithful to you. (28) But as for me, it is good to be near God. I have made the Sovereign Lord my refuge; I will tell of all your deeds.

STUFF TO KNOW Think of this psalm as a romp through four themes:

Verses 2–12 The thundering nastiness of evil people
Verses 13–15 How a good guy or girl feels when evildoers succeed
Verses 16–20 The ugly future of the wicked
Verses 1, 21–28 Why hope in God still makes sense

Scan verses 2–12. Write down at least four facts true of people tall or tiny who are into doing wrong. There's a wad of wise truths, but here are some examples: *Evil people succeed. They have no problems. They are proud of their success. They laugh at God and have no fear of his judgment.*

Evil people seem invincible. But what's their real future? What do verses 16–20 say?

Who guarantees this fate (verses 16–20)?

Asaph admits he was "grieved," "embittered," "senseless," "ignorant" until he saw that God would punish the wicked (verses 1, 21–22). What facts does Asaph discover about God?

BIG QUESTIONS Go back and reread verses 13–15, where Asaph sees this evil and decides it's been stupid to stay out of trouble. Do you agree with him? Why or why not?

Complete this sentence: When I feel like I've been abandoned by my family, friends, and pet hamster, I can depend on . . .

You're in a bad situation. What's your first thought? Circle your pick:

a) It grinds that evil people get away with everything.
b) Evil people are going to get it in the end.
c) I've got God in the meantime.

Trick question. The answer is (d) All of the above. You'll go crazy if you don't honestly reckon with all three facts. The first reaction is honest—and it's also what God thinks. The second reaction is hopeful—it remembers the no-escape destiny of evildoers. And the third reaction is truly helpful—because some days all you've got to cling to is God.

DEEP THOT You need family. You hope for friends. And even when everyone on the planet lets you down, God still hangs on to your hand.

STICKY STUFF There are a bunch of verses in Psalm 73 worth pondering permanently, but there's a card for Psalm 73:25–26 in the back of the book. Remember this: When you feel alone, God is with you.

ACT ON IT Copy Psalm 73:23–28 on a sheet of paper, decorate it, and post it in the loneliest spot in your life—your locker, your math book, wherever.

DIG ON Read Malachi 4:1–3 for a glimpse into how God's people will have a stompin' good time at the end of time.

15. Ketchup Face

The prayer Jesus taught

"I . . . I have to use the rest room," you stammer. "I might be a while. You go ahead and start without me." Your face is quickly as red as the ketchup bottle you're focusing on, trying not to make eye contact with the rest of your table. You escape, scurrying off to the rest room and hoping you can time it just right to avoid yet another embarrassing moment. "We waited, honey," nods your aunt as you return to the table. She grabs your hand, then your cousin's. She stands. She clears her throat. As she yodels thanks to God for your meal with eyes shut tight, you sneak your hand away and slither under the table.

BRAIN DRAIN What is prayer? What's your favorite way to pray? And what bugs you about prayer?

FLASHBACK Jesus has just been talking about what it means to be really spiritual, explaining that people who pump up their religion in front of people just to be seen are, well, losers (Matthew 6:1–4). They're totally unlike people who live a real faith that sometimes happens to show up where people can see it (Matthew 5:14).

BIBLE CHUNK Read Matthew 6:5–13

(5) "And when you pray, do not be like the hypocrites, for they love to pray standing in the synagogues and on the street corners to be seen by men. I tell you the truth, they have received their reward in full. (6) But when you pray, go into your room, close the door and pray to your Father,

who is unseen. Then your Father, who sees what is done in secret, will reward you. (7) And when you pray, do not keep on babbling like pagans, for they think they will be heard because of their many words. (8) Do not be like them, for your Father knows what you need before you ask him.

(9) "This, then, is how you should pray: 'Our Father in heaven, hallowed be your name, (10) your kingdom come, your will be done on earth as it is in heaven. (11) Give us today our daily bread. (12) Forgive us our debts, as we also have forgiven our debtors. (13) And lead us not into temptation, but deliver us from the evil one.' "

STUFF TO KNOW Some people think the only way to pray is long, loud, and lovely—tucking in "thee's" and "thou's" so they sound hyperspiritual. So just in case you're worried you can't pray like a pastor, what does Jesus say prayer *shouldn't* be (verses 5, 7)?

SIDELIGHT Jesus didn't mean you shouldn't ever pray in front of people. After all, Jesus told people to pray in groups (Matthew 18:19–20) and did it here himself. What he didn't want was for people to strut their stuff—to pray to be seen or heard by others.

So why shouldn't you show off when you pray (verse 6)?

God only hears long prayers, right? Why? Or is it why not (verses 7–8)?

When Jesus says, "Hey—this is how you should pray," what everyday stuff does he pray for (verses 9–13)?

INSIGHT Lots to catch in that passage: "Hallowed be your name" asks that God's name would be prized. "Your kingdom come" and "your will be done" both want God's ways worked out on planet earth. "Daily bread" asks God for the things you *need*, not all the stuff you may *want*. "Forgive us our debts" doesn't mean "Lord, pay back the money I borrowed from my little bro's piggy bank," but "Don't hold our *moral* debts against us," like saying "forgive us as we forgive others." And "lead us not into temptation" requests help in overcoming evil.

What can you conclude from this Bible Chunk about how God understands and answers your requests?

INSIGHT You might be wondering whether Matthew misplaced the last line of the "Lord's Prayer" you say in church. The part "For yours is the kingdom and the power and the glory forever. Amen" shows up only in some late copies of Bible manuscripts, so many Bible translations add it as a footnote. But it's still good stuff.

BIG QUESTIONS Who is the best pray-er you know? Why pick that person? Is that how you try to pray?

How do you think you're *supposed* to pray? Is it what Jesus describes?

How do you feel about praying by yourself? How about with other people?

SIDELIGHT Don't ever think you're praying to a grouchy God. God ain't that way. Jesus, in fact, told a wild story about a guy who goes to a friend's house in the middle of the night wanting to borrow bread. "Can't you tell the doors are locked? We're all in bed!" the bugged friend hollers back. If humans can manage to open their doors in the middle of the night, Jesus said, God is truly eager to give. He promised this: "So I say to you: Ask and it will be given to you; seek and you will find; knock and the door will be opened to you" (Luke 11:9).

So what things in your life can you pray for?

What would make prayer easier for you?

DEEP THOT Jesus doesn't expect you to yodel your prayer when you eat out at Billy Bob's Bovine Burger Barn. The religious leaders of his day were teaching that prayer should be loud and long. Jesus shows you what the biggest quality of prayer should be: that it's *real.*

ACT ON IT If you're not keen on praying with other people, find someone who feels the same way—and pray together.

STICKY STUFF You maybe already have this one lodged in your long-term memory: Seeing that Jesus gave you a model prayer, it's not a bad idea to mull and memorize Matthew 6:9–13.

DIG ON Read Ephesians 4:14–21 for some deep stuff to pray for yourself and your friends.

Talk About It • 3

EMPATHIZE: What's going on in your life?
ENCOURAGE: How are you doing with Jesus?
EQUIP: What one truth will you take home today?

- What do your friends think God is like? (Study 11)
- So what's God really like—according to Isaiah 40:21–31? (Study 11)
- What does Hebrews 4:14–16 tell you Jesus is like? (Study 12)
- If God is who the Bible says he is, how do you feel about praying to him? (Study 15)
- What do you need other Christians to do for you? (Study 13)
- What two Christian friends can you call when you need help? (Study 13)
- How does God support you when bad people rule? (Study 14)
- Who do you have when no one else is around? (Study 14)
- Who is Eutychus? (Study 13) What's his claim to fame? (Check out Acts 20:9–10)

PART 4

STAYING CLEAR OF SHARP STICKS

16. Bizarre Believers

The greatest commandment

You can't avoid it: Some people assume that because you're a Christian you're automatically *mucho bizarro*. That fact might have you asking, "Can I be a Christian without being weird?" Jesus doesn't tell you to wear a strange hat, shave your head, or hang out waiting for the end of the world to happen. What makes you different from other people is that you're learning to love God totally and learning to love others unselfishly. Now, *that* really stands out in a crowd.

BRAIN DRAIN What do you think a super spiritually mature Christian looks like—someone who really knows and follows God?

FLASHBACK In this Bible Chunk two groups of religious leaders—the Sadducees and Pharisees—plot to trick Jesus into saying something that would make him look stupid in front of the crowds. The Pharisees weren't fair because they laid lots of rules on people and then did nothing to help lift the load. And the Sadducees were sad, you see, because they didn't believe in the resurrection of the dead (how God raises his people to live with him in heaven forever). The Sadducees also sought political power and influence among leaders, while the Pharisees sought to sway the crowds. Jesus' wise answers to their questions amazed the people (Matthew 22:22, 33).

BIBLE CHUNK Read Matthew 22:34–40

(34) Hearing that Jesus had silenced the Sadducees, the Pharisees got together. (35) One of them, an expert in the law, tested him with this ques-

tion: (36) "Teacher, which is the greatest commandment in the Law?"

(37) Jesus replied: " 'Love the Lord your God with all your heart and with all your soul and with all your mind.' (38) This is the first and greatest commandment. (39) And the second is like it: 'Love your neighbor as yourself.' (40) All the Law and the Prophets hang on these two commandments."

STUFF TO KNOW What drives the Pharisees to quiz Jesus (verse 35)?

What question does the Pharisee pose (verse 36)?

And what does Jesus rattle back (verses 37–38)?

See how the Pharisees ask for one commandment and get two? If Jesus says all the teachings of the Bible "hang on these two commandments," what's so important about these two?

Here's a thought: If you hate the person sitting next to you, then you don't really love God. If you hate God, then your ugliness always spills out on people. You can't separate love for God from love for people. And if you've mastered these two commandments you've mastered all the rest.

SIDELIGHT Jesus knew these leaders were like some church folk. They look totally religious yet miss the point of knowing God. The whole goal of Scripture—"the Law and the Prophets"—is to help you put God first and to love people at least as much as you love yourself. Jesus didn't have much patience for people who look pretty but didn't practice what they preached. Look at Matthew 23 to learn about the seven "woes" Jesus pronounced against them.

BIG QUESTIONS

What would you say is the most important thing about being a Christian?

Okay. You cheated. You just read the Bible Chunk that gives the answer. But what do some people *make* the most important part of being a Christian? Think hard about how people define what a real Christian looks like and scribble a bunch:

INSIGHT

You can find people who rocket all sorts of things to the top of that list. To be a real Christian, they say, you have to drag your bod to church twelve times a week, pray intense and impressive prayers, worship loudly, worship quietly with smells and bells, show off certain spiritual gifts, join the right youth group, go to a Christian school instead of public school, and/or be hyper-precise about the details of Christ's return or other tiny Bible details. Each of those things is fine. Some are downright important. But all are pointless if your faith doesn't start and end with loving God and loving others.

So if loving God is that big a deal, how could your life look when you love God with all your heart?

And what could your life be like if you care about people as much as you care about yourself?

Name one or two things you want to change to put your life in line with God's commands.

INSIGHT Notice that Jesus didn't toss out "the Law and the Prophets." He just summed them up. Your faith won't work without a definition of what love looks like, and all of God's commands and actions in the Bible picture what real-life love looks like. The whole Bible, though, is a pretty big hunk of stuff to learn. In the next four lessons you're going to hit *four majorly important areas* where God wants to remake you.

DEEP THOT "I'm fourteen," you might say. "Isn't this spiritual stuff kind of complicated?" Even if everything else escapes from your brain, God wants you to keep two points straight: love God, love people. That's simple enough.

STICKY STUFF You'll never be dumb about real spiritual stuff as long as you remember Matthew 22:37–39.

ACT ON IT See if you can startle someone who doesn't like Christians by asking *why*. And see if you can do a double startle by *listening* instead of talking.

DIG ON God gave us a tight definition of love in 1 Corinthians 13. Flip open your Bible and read that "love chapter."

17. Cookie Jars and Dumpsters

Stuff to think about

Cookie jars and garbage Dumpsters both have lids. But only one is worth diving in to dine. What's in your head can be sweet or stinkin', depending on what you let live there. One of the first big changes God wants to work in you when you get to know him is rearranging your brain—changing your thoughts so they line up with his.

BRAIN DRAIN Quick: What were you thinking about a minute ago? Fifteen minutes ago? How about yesterday—ten minutes before the end of math?

FLASHBACK Right after this Bible Chunk, Paul says, "Whatever you have learned or received or heard from me, or seen in me—put it into practice. And the God of peace will be with you" (Philippians 4:9). He's saying, "I've tried this. It works. You try it too."

BIBLE CHUNK Read Philippians 4:6–8

> (6) Do not be anxious about anything, but in everything, by prayer and petition, with thanksgiving, present your requests to God. (7) And the peace of God, which transcends all understanding, will guard your hearts and your minds in Christ Jesus.
>
> (8) Finally, brothers, whatever is true, whatever is noble, whatever is right, whatever is pure, whatever is lovely, whatever is admirable—if anything is excellent or praiseworthy—think about such things.

STUFF TO KNOW Some of the stuff you face in life makes you uptight. What can you do besides worry (verse 6)?

DA'SCOOP "Prayer" and "petition" sound like the same thing, like it's saying, "Just ask and ask!" Actually, the word for prayer here refers to worship—telling God he's great. Petition refers to asking—telling your requests to God.

What does thankfulness say about your expectations of God (verse 6)?

God promises something will happen in your heart when you pray this way. What is it (verse 7)?

SIDELIGHT This isn't the only Bible Chunk that promises peace to those who pray. First Peter 5:7 tells you, "Cast all your anxiety on him because he cares for you." And Isaiah 26:3–4 says, "You will keep in perfect peace him whose mind is steadfast, because he trusts in you. Trust in the Lord forever, for the Lord, the Lord, is the Rock eternal."

Worry isn't the only thing in your head that can be out of whack. God wants to replace ugly thoughts with great ones. What good things should be bouncing through your brain (verse 8)?

DA'SCOOP "True" means "valid," "reliable," and "honest." "Noble" is things that "conform to God's standards." "Pure" refers to morally pure, and "lovely" to what is "pleasing" or "agreeable." And "admirable" means what is "praiseworthy," "attractive," and what "rings true to the highest standards."

BIG QUESTIONS No one can see inside your head except you and God. So answer this: What do you worry about when no one is looking?

This Bible Chunk says you can pray instead of puking with worry. Good idea or bad idea?

Suppose you just prayed about a problem. What are you expecting to feel? Instant peace?

SIDELIGHT Peace happens when your life is in line with God. *Prayer doesn't excuse you from action.* You *should* be worried if you're praying for God to do your homework. Solution: Do your best and let God take care of the rest (Proverbs 13:4). *Prayer is all about trust.* It's possible to pray for a good thing and have an evil backup plan if God doesn't show up. In that case, he won't. Solution: Check your motives (James 1:5–8). *Prayer is asking for God's walloping best, not your whims.* Prayer isn't a magical miracle fix. You're inviting God to act in your life as he sees fit (Romans 8:28).

Worry isn't the only out-of-whack thing maybe going on in your mind. What is Paul saying *not* to think about?

You maybe never think about the thoughts in your head. But how close do you come to the standard Paul gives in verse 8? Rate the value of your brain activity.

My brain is a sewer. My brain is sweet

SIDELIGHT A brain change doesn't happen automatically. First Thessalonians 5:21 says you need to "test everything. Hold on to the good." You push bad stuff out of your brain by replacing it with good.

What clean stuff—hobbies, helping people, homework—can you fill your mind with?

DEEP THOT Some days you might feel like a chicken running around the yard with your head chopped off, living on pure reflex. But God intends you to be a thoughtful person. You might think that what goes on in your own private mind can't hurt anybody. Yet what you think determines how you feel and how you act. And your actions—well, they can either hurt or help you and others.

STICKY STUFF Keep in mind what you should keep in mind: Philippians 4:8.

ACT ON IT Set your watch or another alarm to go off in an hour. When it dings write down what you're thinking about. See if you spot any of these: hatred, jealousy, lust, envy, put-downs, meanness, racism, despair, frustration, anger. Or is there good stuff going on?

DIG ON Read 2 Corinthians 10:2–5 to find out how you can take control of your thoughts.

18. Tongue-Tied

Kind words

People know you by what you say and what you do. So figure on this: What flies out of your mouth is half of what people know about you—more than half if you're a big blabberer. Get this: You can't claim you love the people around you if you're always trashing them with your tongue, letting things leap past your lips that are tacky, tasteless, or terrorizing. When God wants to change you, he starts in your head. But getting your tongue tamed is another big change he wants to work in you.

BRAIN DRAIN When words get nasty are you usually the slammer—or the sufferer?

FLASHBACK This Bible Chunk on taming the tongue comes right after some strong teaching on living up to what you claim to believe—and right before a section on how wise people don't use their brains to bash others. Sounds like the tongue is tiny but tremendously important.

BIBLE CHUNK Read James 3:1–12

> (1) Not many of you should presume to be teachers, my brothers, because you know that we who teach will be judged more strictly. (2) We all stumble in many ways. If anyone is never at fault in what he says, he is a perfect man, able to keep his whole body in check.
>
> (3) When we put bits into the mouths of horses to make them obey us, we can turn the whole animal. (4) Or take ships as an example. Although they are so large and are driven by strong winds, they are steered by a very small rudder wherever the pilot wants to go. (5) Likewise the tongue is a

small part of the body, but it makes great boasts. Consider what a great forest is set on fire by a small spark. (6) The tongue also is a fire, a world of evil among the parts of the body. It corrupts the whole person, sets the whole course of his life on fire, and is itself set on fire by hell.

(7) All kinds of animals, birds, reptiles and creatures of the sea are being tamed and have been tamed by man, (8) but no man can tame the tongue. It is a restless evil, full of deadly poison.

(9) With the tongue we praise our Lord and Father, and with it we curse men, who have been made in God's likeness. (10) Out of the same mouth come praise and cursing. My brothers, this should not be. (11) Can both fresh water and salt water flow from the same spring? (12) My brothers, can a fig tree bear olives, or a grapevine bear figs? Neither can a salt spring produce fresh water.

STUFF TO KNOW If you're a teacher—someone who claims to know enough to instruct someone else—then it's true: Everyone is looking at you. What is the person who never messes up in what he or she says (verse 2)?

DA'SCOOP "Stumble" doesn't just mean to mess up, but to sin. There's a mountain of ways we can sin, but we're all prone to sin in what we say.

What's the big deal about a bit or a rudder? What can these small things accomplish (verses 3–4)?

How is that like the tongue (verse 5)?

Verse 6 says the tongue can set life ablaze—and that the evil of the tongue comes from hell itself. Yikes! When have you uttered one of those "sparks" that started a forest fire? Anytime recently?

SIDELIGHT While this Bible Chunk focuses on how most of our mouths are hot enough to char toast, check out this test for all the good your words can do: "Do not let any unwholesome talk come out of your mouths, but only what is helpful for building others up according to their needs, that it may benefit those who listen" (Ephesians 4:29).

If it's easier to clamp shut the jaws of an alligator than to control what you say, is it hopeless to try (verses 7–8)?

So why try? See if you can pull a solution from verses 9–12.

BIG QUESTIONS Think of a time you said something hurtful you had to undo later. What happened?

Did the damage you inflicted make you muzzle your mouth? Why or why not?

What's the best way you've come up with to keep your tongue tied?

SIDELIGHT This Bible Chunk hints in verses 9–12 at a solution to misbehaving mouths. The problem, James says, comes from inside. Jesus said it even more clearly: "The mouth speaks the things that are in the heart" (Matthew 12:34 NCV). If you want to change what comes out of your mouth, you need to change what goes on in your heart.

Can you think of any ugly thoughts that you give so much space in your brain that they can't help but wind up coming out in your words?

DEEP THOT Just because you think a nasty thought doesn't mean you should say it. So it's a start to stifle those sick words. But you're making bigger progress when you start to think differently. Ask God to clean your heart of ugly stuff so it doesn't spew out in what you say.

STICKY STUFF Use Ephesians 4:29 as a measure of your words and you'll always have something worth saying.

ACT ON IT Keep track of your tongue for a day. How many nasty things do you say each day? Take a guess, then keep track tomorrow. The object isn't to see how *many* nasty things you can say but how *few*—and to notice how hard it is to put a leash on that wild thing inside your mouth. How much of what you say would make it past an Ephesians 4:29 loudmouth detector?

DIG ON Read James 3:13–18, where it's obvious that good words come from a pure heart.

19. A Stick in Your Eye

Revenge

You gotta wonder if Jesus ever got beat up on the playground. After all, he's the guy who said "Love your enemies" (Matthew 5:44) and "Turn the other cheek" (Matthew 5:39). Yet one thing shows for sure that Jesus was no wuss: He was radically tough in his willingness to suffer for others' sake.

God wants to grab hold of your head. He wants to tame your tongue. And here's a third big change God wants to work in you: He aims to alter you to behave like Jesus when you wander out into the big mean thing called life.

BRAIN DRAIN How do you defend yourself when people hurt you?

FLASHBACK Jesus' friend and follower Peter wrote this next Bible Chunk to slaves (see 1 Peter 2:18). Slavery back in Bible times wasn't what it was in the United States before the Civil War; slaves had families, and people often sold themselves into slavery—for a time—to get ahead. Even so, if your master was nasty, life was hard. The job of a Christian slave was to submit and be loyal, even when a master was harsh. Sound tough? For sure. But wait till you hear what Jesus endured.

BIBLE CHUNK Read 1 Peter 2:19–25

(19) For it is commendable if a man bears up under the pain of unjust suffering because he is conscious of God. (20) But how is it to your credit if you receive a beating for doing wrong and endure it? But if you suffer

for doing good and you endure it, this is commendable before God. (21) To this you were called, because Christ suffered for you, leaving you an example, that you should follow in his steps. (22) "He committed no sin, and no deceit was found in his mouth." (23) When they hurled their insults at him, he did not retaliate; when he suffered, he made no threats. Instead, he entrusted himself to him who judges justly. (24) He himself bore our sins in his body on the tree, so that we might die to sins and live for righteousness; by his wounds you have been healed. (25) For you were like sheep going astray, but now you have returned to the Shepherd and Overseer of your souls.

STUFF TO KNOW What's it mean to suffer unjustly? What are you supposed to do when that happens (verses 19–20)?

How was Jesus' suffering big-time unfair (verse 22)?

What sort of suffering did he endure (verses 23–24)?

SIDELIGHT Jesus knew what it felt like to be on the receiving end of abuse you no way deserve. That's different, Peter says, from getting what you've got coming for being bad. The word for "beating," by the way, means "strike with the fist." It's used in Mark 14:65 for how Christ was tortured at his trial.

How did Jesus react to evil (verses 23–24)?

In the end, what happened to Jesus (verse 24)?

So what good did it do for Jesus to suffer (verses 24–25)?

When Jesus suffered, he *didn't* do four things and *did* do one. What were they (verses 22–23)?

BIG QUESTIONS Sticks and stones break your bones—and a stick in your eye hurts even worse. But you're not supposed to strike back. What do you think about letting insults bounce off and suffering gladly?

What good does it do you to know God is watching out for you when you bang heads or get beat up?

SIDELIGHT Get this: Jesus was strategic about his suffering, giving his life when it really mattered. Jesus was known to ditch the guys who wanted to do him in (Matthew 12:14–15). But when it came time to die on the cross, he didn't call an army of angels to save him (Matthew 26:53). He embraced the cross (Hebrews 12:2). And he purposely laid down his life (John 10:17–18).

So what does all that say about when you should choose to suffer—instead of pounding back with the same kind of punch that hit you?

Look back at those four things Jesus *didn't* do and the one thing he *did* do from verses 22–23. How well does that approach work in your world?

What's happened in your life when you haven't handled tough stuff that way?

Think of one situation right now where someone is messing with your mind, talking behind your back, or spitting in your soda. What can you change in how you react?

DEEP THOT Jesus doesn't expect you to be stupid about suffering. If you're the victim of violence or bullying, you need to run for help to an adult you trust. And Jesus knows all about the everyday evil you can get in return for your kindness. Jesus never volunteered to get the tar beat out of him. But he gladly suffered when the time was right.

STICKY STUFF Tuck 1 Peter 2:23 between your ears for your next bout of tough times.

ACT ON IT In Romans 12:21 Paul said some stuff similar to what Peter had to say: "Do not be overcome by evil, but overcome evil with good." Try that on someone today.

DIG ON Read Romans 12:17–21 for the scoop on the best way to heap burning coals on your enemies' heads.

20. Nuclear Toaster

God's plan for love and sex

Even over the phone you could notice Becka's nose wrinkling with disgust. "Nick's too pure," she tells you. "I can't imagine him as my boyfriend. I can't imagine him as anyone's boyfriend. Kissing him would be like . . . *bleeehhck* . . . kissing my brother."

If you're giving your brain, your talk, and your every action to God—three big changes—then you can trust your lips and the rest of your body to him too—because it all belongs to him. Allowing God to steer your love life is big change number four God wants to do to you.

BRAIN DRAIN No giggles, please: How have your views of the opposite sex changed in the past four years?

FLASHBACK This Bible Chunk is from Paul's letter to the people in Thessolonica. He couldn't get any gushier as he congratulated them on their faith. He tells them God's Good News came to them "not simply with words, but also with power"; they "became imitators of us and of the Lord"; in spite of severe suffering they "welcomed the message with the joy given by the Holy Spirit"; and they "became a model to all the believers" (1 Thessalonians 1:5–8). Paul's praise is pointed and abundant, but look at what huge point he makes when he urges them to grow even more.

BIBLE CHUNK 1 Thessalonians 4:1–8

(1) Finally, brothers, we instructed you how to live in order to please God, as in fact you are living. Now we ask you and urge you in the Lord

Jesus to do this more and more. (2) For you know what instructions we gave you by the authority of the Lord Jesus.

(3) It is God's will that you should be sanctified: that you should avoid sexual immorality; (4) that each of you should learn to control his own body in a way that is holy and honorable, (5) not in passionate lust like the heathen, who do not know God; (6) and that in this matter no one should wrong his brother or take advantage of him. The Lord will punish men for all such sins, as we have already told you and warned you. (7) For God did not call us to be impure, but to live a holy life. (8) Therefore, he who rejects this instruction does not reject man but God, who gives you his Holy Spirit.

STUFF TO KNOW What's Paul's attitude toward the Thessalonians? Does it sound like they have huge problems (verses 1–2)?

So what topic does he pick to teach these spiritually intense people?

INSIGHT Just a year or two before Paul wrote, major leaders of the early church had gathered in Jerusalem to decide major points to teach new Christians. They issued two important instructions. One was that believers must flee sexual sin (Acts 15:22–35). In other words, out of a world of issues they could have fretted over, they singled out sex as really important.

DA'SCOOP When the Bible says it's God's will that you be "sanctified," it means he wants you wholly dedicated to him. "Sexual immorality" is another way of saying sexual sin. And "heathens," like the verse says, are people who don't know God.

What does Paul say sanctification—that deep dedication to God—looks like (verses 4–5)?

SIDELIGHT The kind of purity God wants to put inside you doesn't just show up in behavior ("avoid sexual immorality"). It's also about attitudes ("passionate lust"). Lust is hot pursuit of something you can't have—whether it's the right thing in the wrong time or just plain the wrong thing. God's got all the bases covered.

God is no prude. He thunk up the whole sex thing. And he never makes a rule without a reason. So who all gets hurt by sexual immorality (verse 6)?

INSIGHT The point about "wronging" a brother or "taking advantage" is that lots of people suffer the effects of sexual messes—not just the couple involved but their present or future mates.

Is all this boundary-setting just Paul's idea? Or who's coming up with the commands (verse 8)?

BIG QUESTIONS You might know God's rules for sex. But knowing rules and following them can be two wildly opposite deals. What do you think about what the Bible says about sexual boundaries—how Christians should pursue purity in both brain and body?

Is what you want out of sex and relationships going God's way—or getting looser? Why?

SIDELIGHT God's goal isn't to dunk all your bodily desires in ice. He wants them to heat up when and where he intended.

God made sex hotter than a nuclear-powered toaster. But he made it for sharing between a husband and wife. It's part of his plan for them to experience physical and emotional union (Genesis 2:22–24 and Hebrews 13:4).

What sorts of things in your life are influencing you away from God's best for sex?

SIDELIGHT You have to make a choice not to feed on things that heat you up outside God's plan. Guys often get going from what they see—including unhelpful and unholy stuff like pornography, sweaty videos, and the dim corners of the Internet. Girls often grow wrong desires when they set their dreams, wishes, and affection on the wrong guy. Jesus had a simple solution for everything that can make you stumble: Get rid of it (Matthew 5:27–30).

DEEP THOT Sex inside marriage is God's best. Run away from the rest: Sex isn't for people not married to each other. It isn't a party game, a dare, or a contest to get as much as you can. The sex God invented isn't selfish, hurtful, violent, or controlling. Sex isn't something adults or teens do to children or for people of the same sex. Sex isn't a spectator sport for the screen or magazine. Decide now: Do you want God's best? If not, you're going to slide into the rest.

STICKY STUFF Put 1 Thessalonians 4:3–4 in your pocket and stay pure.

ACT ON IT Write a letter to yourself committing to staying pure—starting with the boundaries you set. List reasons why in the middle, and end with what you're going to do to stay pure if temptation feels like it's too much.

DIG ON Think God knows nothing about sex? Read Proverbs 5:15–23 to find out what he really thinks about his great gift to you.

Talk About It • 4

EMPATHIZE: What's going on in your life?
ENCOURAGE: How are you doing with Jesus?
EQUIP: What one truth will you take home today?

- If you walked up to a crowd on the street and asked people to name the most important part of being a Christian, what would they say? (Study 16)
- What would you say is the biggest thing about being a Christian? (Study 16)
- How does God want to rearrange your brain—to change the way you think? (Study 17)
- What do you expect from God when you pray? How realistic are your expectations? (Study 17)
- Think of a time you said something hurtful you had to undo later. What happened? (Study 18)
- Where do ugly words really come from? (Study 18)
- How did Jesus react to evil? Was his approach a good idea or bad idea? (Study 19)
- How about those four things Jesus didn't do and one thing he did in 1 Peter 2:22–23? How well does that approach work in your world? (Study 19)
- Is God a prude? (Study 20)
- What's it mean to want God's best plan for sex? (Study 20)

PART 5

BUILDING ON THE ROCK

21. Bad Boy Bart

The fruit of the Spirit

You don't get away from being bad by trying harder, by making promises and resolutions, or by telling God you cross your heart and hope he doesn't strike you dead if you ever do *that* again. Little-known factoid: Bart Simpson didn't get even a booger better by writing rules on the blackboard: "I will not conduct my own fire drills." "The principal's toupee is not a Frisbee." "I will not do that thing with my tongue." "I will not burp in class." Or even "I will not do anything bad ever again." God is way brighter than Bart's teacher when it comes to remaking people.

BRAIN DRAIN What's your most pesky struggle as a Christian? If you don't want to write it here, tell God about it. Actually, you can do that anyway.

FLASHBACK The people in Galatia who got this letter had been fooled into thinking that they could make themselves right with God by being good—and that they could be better people without God's help. For the last couple chapters they've been hearing truly good news: "Don't get stuck in endless lists of rules. Don't waste your life on empty rituals. Don't play church." Now Paul is about to tell them the real way to get free from their old habits of sin.

BIBLE CHUNK Read Galatians 5:13–26

> (13) You, my brothers, were called to be free. But do not use your freedom to indulge the sinful nature; rather, serve one another in love.

(14) The entire law is summed up in a single command: "Love your neighbor as yourself." (15) If you keep on biting and devouring each other, watch out or you will be destroyed by each other.

(16) So I say, live by the Spirit, and you will not gratify the desires of the sinful nature. (17) For the sinful nature desires what is contrary to the Spirit, and the Spirit what is contrary to the sinful nature. They are in conflict with each other, so that you do not do what you want. (18) But if you are led by the Spirit, you are not under law.

(19) The acts of the sinful nature are obvious: sexual immorality, impurity and debauchery; (20) idolatry and witchcraft; hatred, discord, jealousy, fits of rage, selfish ambition, dissensions, factions (21) and envy; drunkenness, orgies, and the like. I warn you, as I did before, that those who live like this will not inherit the kingdom of God.

(22) But the fruit of the Spirit is love, joy, peace, patience, kindness, goodness, faithfulness, (23) gentleness and self-control. Against such things there is no law. (24) Those who belong to Christ Jesus have crucified the sinful nature with its passions and desires. (25) Since we live by the Spirit, let us keep in step with the Spirit. (26) Let us not become conceited, provoking and envying each other.

STUFF TO KNOW Spiritually, you're freer than free. You're forgiven. Forever! You're God's friend. Forever! What does Paul say *not* to do with your freedom (verse 13)?

INSIGHT When Paul says not to indulge your "sinful nature," he means to not give in to all the bad stuff you're capable of apart from God jamming his hand into your life in Jesus. The sinful nature is the "old you" that can still get ugly.

If you're not supposed to live in sin, what do you do with all your free time (verses 13–14)? And what happens if you don't rid yourself of old stuff (verse 15)?

What kind of help do you expect from God in getting spiritually grown-up (verse 16)?

SIDELIGHT Paul doesn't say a lot here about *how* the Holy Spirit will work in your life—just that he will. Other places in the Bible say that God the Spirit changes you from the inside out by washing you clean and giving you a new birth (Titus 3:5), teaching you (John 14:26), empowering you (Acts 1:8), giving you a spiritual gift (1 Corinthians 12:7), teaching you truth (John 16:14), and continuing to fill you (Ephesians 5:17). Spiritual growth isn't magic. It's a relationship.

How do the desires of the Spirit and the desires of your old sinfulness get along? Are they buddies (verse 17)?

What sorts of nasty attitudes and actions result from the sinful nature (verses 19–21)?

What does Paul say about people who "live like this" (verse 21)?

SIDELIGHT As you grow in Christ, the new you gets stronger than the old, sinful you—but you still won't ever outgrow your need to choose God's way and to depend on him. You won't get perfect (remember 1 John 1 and 2?). But you get way better. Read Romans 8 for more.

What great things result from the Spirit? Jot down the nine "fruit of the Spirit" (verses 22–23).

BIG QUESTIONS How do you expect your faith and obedience to get bigger and stronger? What does God do in you—and what do you do?

INSIGHT The Spirit has given you new life. Now you need to "keep in step" and stay close. It's like going for a walk. God is God, so he gets to pick the path. But every time he takes a step, you have a choice to take the same step—or to walk the other way (verse 25). When you walk with him and get to know him, you start to look like him.

This Bible Chunk contains a pile of negative things and a pile of positive things. What do you want to get rid of? What do you want to grab hold of?

DEEP THOT When you became a Christian, God started something in you. Through forgiveness you got a fresh friendship. Staying close to him through the Holy Spirit sounds simple, but going step by step is the secret of growth.

STICKY STUFF Think about God's good stuff. Memorize Galatians 5:22–23.

ACT ON IT God always answers a prayer that asks to grow: Ask him to work in you by his Spirit, to strengthen you through his Word, and to make you wholly devoted to him.

DIG ON Give these passages a read to learn more about the Spirit's work in you: Romans 8 and Titus 3:5–7.

22. Buy the Book

Why you can buy the Bible

Sooner or later you get it shoved in your face: "You only believe the Bible because you don't know anything else." Or "You believe the Bible because your parents and pastor tell you to." Or "You're stupid to think the Bible is any better than any other book." God's Word doesn't just make you strong. It also makes you smart. But you have to decide first if you believe it.

BRAIN DRAIN Why do you buy the Bible? What do you say to people who don't?

FLASHBACK Only a few years earlier, Paul had been under house arrest in Rome—the time when he wrote the Bible books of Titus and 1 Timothy. Now he was in prison again, hidden from his friends in a cold dungeon. Paul knew his life was nearly done (2 Timothy 4:6–8), and he wanted his young friend Timothy to know why he should continue on as a Christian even though he knew Paul was suffering.

BIBLE CHUNK Read 2 Timothy 3:10–4:5

(3:10) You, however, know all about my teaching, my way of life, my purpose, faith, patience, love, endurance, (3:11) persecutions, sufferings—what kinds of things happened to me in Antioch, Iconium and Lystra, the persecutions I endured. Yet the Lord rescued me from all of them. (3:12) In fact, everyone who wants to live a godly life in Christ Jesus will be persecuted, (3:13) while evil men and impostors will go from bad to worse, deceiving and being deceived (3:14). But as for you, continue in what you have learned and have become convinced of, because you know those from whom you learned it, (3:15) and how from infancy you have known the holy Scriptures, which are able to make you wise for salvation through faith in Christ Jesus. (3:16) All Scripture is God-breathed and is useful for teaching, rebuking, correcting and training in righteousness (3:17), so that the man of God may be thoroughly equipped for every good work.

(4:1) In the presence of God and of Christ Jesus, who will judge the living and the dead, and in view of his appearing and his kingdom, I give you this charge: (4:2) Preach the Word; be prepared in season and out of season; correct, rebuke and encourage—with great patience and careful instruction. (4:3) For the time will come when men will not put up with sound doctrine. Instead, to suit their own desires, they will gather around them a great number of teachers to say what their itching ears want to hear. (4:4) They will turn their ears away from the truth and turn aside to myths. (4:5) But you, keep your head in all situations, endure hardship, do the work of an evangelist, discharge all the duties of your ministry.

STUFF TO KNOW Why does Paul tell Timothy to believe the faith—to continue in what he has learned and become convinced is true (verses 3:14–15)? Jot down both reasons.

Paul says *he* is one reason. Go back and look at how Paul describes himself in verses 3:10–12. What about Paul is convincing?

Who is Paul *not* like (verse 3:13)?

SIDELIGHT There's more to Paul's story than he says here. God had worked a 180-degree reversal in Paul, who at one point helped kill Christians because he thought it was the cool thing to do (Galatians 1:13). Paul isn't the only person who has taught Timothy the Bible. Timothy would have formally studied Scripture from age five. More than that, he also learned from his grandmother Lois and his mother, Lydia (2 Timothy 1:5).

Look at this Bible Chunk like this: *Faces*—the people who wrote the Bible, and who teach it to you—are the first reason the Bible is believable. The *facts* of what the Bible is and does are reason number two. Where did the Bible come from (verse 3:16)?

What is the Bible able to do (verses 3:15–17)?

SIDELIGHT This Bible chunk says *where* the Bible came from—it's God-breathed—as in straight from God. Another place—2 Peter 1:21—says more on exactly *how* God inspired the Bible. People didn't make it up, "men spoke from God as they were carried along by the Holy Spirit."

What does Paul tell Timothy to do with what he knows (verses 4:1–2)?

So what does Paul predict will happen if Timothy does what he should (verses 4:3–4)?

BIG QUESTIONS That Bible Chunk doesn't end on the cheeriest note. Lots of people won't believe the true message of God contained in the Bible. So what makes the Bible believable to you? Or what parts are hard to swallow?

Paul says *facts* and *faces* make the Bible credible. Does that convince you? Why or why not?

SIDELIGHT Those lots of people who say you're clueless to believe the Bible don't have a clue what they're talking about. Let the Bible respond for itself to these biggie slams: *Believing in God is for wimps.* (Second Corinthians 11:23–27—Read Paul's diary. He wasn't weak.) *There are a lot of other good religions. Jesus was just another teacher.* (John 14:6—Jesus claimed to be the only way.) *Christians are hypocrites—they always say one thing and do another.* (Isaiah 29:13–14—God hates hypocrites.) *The Bible is full of myths.* (Second Timothy 3:16—Ask them to name specific myths or points where history contradicts the Bible.) *God can't exist because I've never gotten an answer to prayer.* (Psalm 14:1—God's reality isn't limited to our knowledge of him.)

DEEP THOT You won't trust the Bible to steer your life if you can't swallow what it says—either how it tells you to live or how it presents the facts that God exists, loves the world he made, and wants to be your friend. You gotta buy the Book.

STICKY STUFF Hold on tight to 2 Timothy 3:16 for truth about where the Bible comes from.

ACT ON IT Find someone who knows the Bible better than you and quiz her or him on the Bible's trustworthiness. There's no question someone hasn't asked—and had answered.

DIG ON Check out those verses listed above to find out how well the Bible answers all the questions you can throw at it.

23. The Gigantical Quizzical *Why?*

Be prepared to explain your faith

"So why *do* you believe in God?" she quizzed you. You'd had nightmares about getting cornered with that question by some believer-bashing lunatic—and without your Sunday school teacher by your side. Or about seeing every head in science class do a slow-motion turn to watch your teacher torture you—all for losing a brain-to-brain debate of the scientific merits of creation. But this—this was your best friend, asking a simple question you wished you had a smooth answer for. With her parents going through a divorce, your friend was questioning everything she thought she believed. And she needed to know how you could still think God cared. *"Really!"* cried her eyes. "I want to *know*."

BRAIN DRAIN Has anyone ever asked you why you're a Christian—or pushed you to defend what you believe? What happened?

FLASHBACK A few pages back you read Peter's advice on how to face suffering like Jesus did: committing no sin, telling no lies, throwing no punches, and lobbing no threats. In this Bible Chunk Peter builds on those points and tosses in another: Getting tormented can be a chance to tell people about Jesus.

BIBLE CHUNK Read 1 Peter 3:8–17

(8) Finally, all of you, live in harmony with one another; be sympathetic, love as brothers, be compassionate and humble. (9) Do not repay evil with evil or insult with insult, but with blessing, because to this you were called so that you may inherit a blessing. (10) For, "Whoever would love life and see good days must keep his tongue from evil and his lips from deceitful speech. (11) He must turn from evil and do good; he must seek peace and pursue it. (12) For the eyes of the Lord are on the righteous and his ears are attentive to their

prayer, but the face of the Lord is against those who do evil."

(13) Who is going to harm you if you are eager to do good? (14) But even if you should suffer for what is right, you are blessed. "Do not fear what they fear; do not be frightened." (15) But in your hearts set apart Christ as Lord. Always be prepared to give an answer to everyone who asks you to give the reason for the hope that you have. But do this with gentleness and respect, (16) keeping a clear conscience, so that those who speak maliciously against your good behavior in Christ may be ashamed of their slander. (17) It is better, if it is God's will, to suffer for doing good than for doing evil.

STUFF TO KNOW So what kind of life are Christians to live? Jot a half dozen biggies from verses 8–12.

What reason do you have to behave (verse 12)?

INSIGHT Peter wonders who is going to harm you if you're eager to do good. Before you start making a list, read the next verse. Peter follows up his hopeful question with some info on what to do when people hurt you despite your niceness.

Fill in the blank: When you suffer for doing right, you are ________ (verse 14). What two things can you do when you're so fortunate (verse 15)?

SIDELIGHT You may not *feel* blessed—especially since "blessed" means "happy." But you *are*. When you know who's in charge—that Christ is Lord—you can stay sane. God's eyes are aimed at you, his ears tuned in to your trouble.

When you're a Christian you've got good stuff inside. What's the best way to spread it around (verse 15)?

SIDELIGHT Jesus always made sharing faith sound normal. Natural. Not nasty. Look at these two big teachings: In Matthew 28:19–20 Jesus said *what* you should do: "Therefore go and make disciples of all nations, baptizing them in the name of the Father and of the Son and of the Holy Spirit, and teaching them to obey everything I have commanded you. And surely I will be with you always, to the very end of the age." That's called "The Great Commission." And in Acts 1:8 he made a "Great Prediction" of *how* and *where* his people would do that: "But you will receive power when the Holy Spirit comes on you; and you will be my witnesses in Jerusalem, and in all Judea and Samaria, and to the ends of the earth."

BIG QUESTIONS Instant replay: Name three things you would say to someone who asks, "Why do you believe in God?" or "Why do you follow Jesus?"

What evidence could you offer from how you live—stuff so convincing "that those who speak maliciously against your good behavior in Christ may be ashamed of their slander" (verse 16)?

Suppose you did live exactly like it says in verses 8–12. What would everybody around you think?

Does that tantalizing prospect make you want to live God's way—or do life your own way?

SIDELIGHT Paul said that Christians are like letters "known and read by everybody" (2 Corinthians 3:2). You "witness" to the goodness and greatness of Jesus not just by what you say but by how you live.

Have you ever made someone mad by sharing your faith minus the "gentleness and reverence"? Who? When? How? Details! Could you undo your boo-boo?

Peter seems to connect suffering and sharing your faith—in other words, that you should share your faith with people who have been less than kind to you. Is he crazy?

DEEP THOT Being friends with God is too good to keep to yourself. It affects your attitudes. It moves out into your actions. And then it splashes out on other people. Whether you're just getting started with God or you've been a Christian a long time, don't hide what you have. There's a world waiting for it.

STICKY STUFF You'll always be prepared if you put 1 Peter 3:15 in your head.

ACT ON IT Think of a friend you'd like to tell about Jesus. Go back and look at *problem-solution-response* (study 7). Think about how *facts* and *faces* make the Bible believable (study 22). Wrap that up in what Jesus means to you, and you've got an explanation of the hope inside you. Share it gently.

DIG ON Read Acts 2:14–41 for the early disciples' first shot at sharing Jesus. It went pretty well.

24. Splish, Slash

Building on the Rock

She was your youngest-ever, funnest-ever Sunday school teacher. Last year you and a swarm of her students all watched her get married, though you did all stay away from the reception so as to not run up the bill. But now—now she's getting a divorce. When you and some friends called her and asked her to grab coffee with you, she said she was uncomfortable talking. And she said she wasn't interested in what you, God, or anyone else at church had to say about her life.

BRAIN DRAIN What do you expect your relationship with God to be like ten years from now? Why?

FLASHBACK Matthew 5–7—the famous Sermon on the Mount—is where Jesus taught his disciples to pray. It's also where Jesus said to love your enemies, turn the other cheek, and chop off anything that yanks you away from God. When Jesus finished preaching, his listeners were amazed. Unlike all the religious leaders around him, he taught with "authority," the power that comes from knowing truth firsthand (Matthew 7:28–29). And to wrap up that significant speech, this Bible Chunk is what he said. Drum roll, please . . .

BIBLE CHUNK Read Matthew 7:13–27

(13) "Enter through the narrow gate. For wide is the gate and broad is the road that leads to destruction, and many enter through it. (14) But

small is the gate and narrow the road that leads to life, and only a few find it.

(15) "Watch out for false prophets. They come to you in sheep's clothing, but inwardly they are ferocious wolves. (16) By their fruit you will recognize them. Do people pick grapes from thornbushes, or figs from thistles? (17) Likewise every good tree bears good fruit, but a bad tree bears bad fruit. (18) A good tree cannot bear bad fruit, and a bad tree cannot bear good fruit. (19) Every tree that does not bear good fruit is cut down and thrown into the fire. (20) Thus, by their fruit you will recognize them.

(21) "Not everyone who says to me, 'Lord, Lord,' will enter the kingdom of heaven, but only he who does the will of my Father who is in heaven. (22) Many will say to me on that day, 'Lord, Lord, did we not prophesy in your name, and in your name drive out demons and perform many miracles?' (23) Then I will tell them plainly, 'I never knew you. Away from me, you evildoers!'

(24) "Therefore everyone who hears these words of mine and puts them into practice is like a wise man who built his house on the rock. (25) The rain came down, the streams rose, and the winds blew and beat against that house; yet it did not fall, because it had its foundation on the rock. (26) But everyone who hears these words of mine and does not put them into practice is like a foolish man who built his house on sand. (27) The rain came down, the streams rose, and the winds blew and beat against that house, and it fell with a great crash."

STUFF TO KNOW

Know it or not, your life is a trip—a search for life. You only get to pick between two paths. How many people hike the wide road? Where's it lead (verse 13)?

Jesus said it's easy to locate the path to destruction because it's packed with people—yet there's always room for one more. If you're looking for the popular path, it looks right. Should you expect a crowd on the skinny road? Where does that road get you (verse 13)?

Loads of people try to point you down what they deem the right path. A false prophet is anyone who seems like a steady guide but isn't. If a bad prophet looks like a cuddly sheep, how can you spot his or her fangs (verse 16)?

What's to keep you from thinking a misleading voice is worth listening to (verses 17–20)?

INSIGHT People can sound good and even display what looks like high-voltage spiritual power. But the word "lord" means "master." And if "Lord" is on their lips without Jesus being king of their heart, it doesn't matter how brilliant, gifted, or spiritual they seem. All that matters is that Jesus is really their master.

Who gets into the kingdom of heaven? Who doesn't (verses 21–23)?

SIDELIGHT The only folks with an entrance pass to heaven are those who do God's will. Remember what the Father wants from us? It's to believe in Christ (John 6:29). Doing God's will starts with trust, not with trying to impress him with your goodness. Once you've got real faith, though, you inevitably grow gobs of real-life obedience.

Some people build life on a foundation other than God. What happens to them (verses 26–27)? What does Jesus call them (verse 26)?

BIG QUESTIONS You're on that spiritual trek. Which path have you picked for your life? How do you know?

Who are you listening to who isn't leading you the right way?

This grand finale to Jesus' Sermon on the Mount says people whose spiritual lives crash and burn neglect to "do the will of the father," to "put these things into practice," and to check if they're bearing genuine "good fruit." They don't build their lives on the one and only right foundation.

So here's the pointed question: What's your life built on? Circle where you stand:

I'm Building on Me (Sand)	*I'm Building on God (Rock)*
My own goodness	God's forgiveness in Christ
My choices	God's commands
My popularity	God's honor
My stuff	God's spiritual treasure

DEEP THOT Splish, splash—eternity is no place to be takin' a bath. A life built on anything less than Jesus crashes faster than a house skids down a mountain in a mud slide.

STICKY STUFF Lots to think about here. Matthew 7:24–25 fills you in on how Jesus would write a building code.

ACT ON IT Ask a mature Christian about people they know who've ditched God. What happened? What's the lesson?

DIG ON Read Psalm 1 to find out more on how smart it is to build your life on God.

25. Job Number One

Friends to follow God with

Your school counselor stares blankly at you. "I know it's hard to understand," you explain. "I'm interested in all this career-day stuff, but I'm also trying to figure out what *God* wants me to do."

"Well, aren't you just a little Mahatma Gandhi," she grins, flashing a smile saved for humoring crazy people. "Or is it Martin Luther King? Or maybe Malcolm X?"

"Actually," you explain, "I'm just trying to follow Jesus. Whatever I do with my life, I just want to stay close to God and be useful to him. For me, that's my first job."

BRAIN DRAIN How are you going to keep getting closer to God now that you've finished *Get God*?

FLASHBACK Timothy was a young man when Paul wrote him the letter that became the Bible book 1 Timothy. A few years later Paul sent Timothy a second letter. While Paul is high on Timothy's faith, he knows other people are wandering from God. Paul tells Tim two truths that will help him stick close to God: "The Lord knows those who are his" and "Everyone who confesses the name of the Lord must turn away from wickedness" (2 Timothy 2:19). And then he adds this Chunk.

BIBLE CHUNK Read 2 Timothy 2:20–22. The "articles" in verse 20 are pots and jars and dishes.

> (20) In a large house there are articles not only of gold and silver, but also of wood and clay; some are for noble purposes and some for ignoble. (21) If a man cleanses himself from the latter, he will be an instrument for

noble purposes, made holy, useful to the Master and prepared to do any good work. (22) Flee the evil desires of youth, and pursue righteousness, faith, love and peace, along with those who call on the Lord out of a pure heart.

STUFF TO KNOW Paul wrote from prison, but he still knows his way around a well-stocked pantry. What kind of dishes are around in a big house (verse 20)?

DA'SCOOP Sounds stuffy—like only the good china ever gets to come out and play. The New Living Translation makes "noble" and "ignoble" more understandable: "The expensive utensils are used for special occasions, and the cheap ones are for everyday use."

This Bible Chunk isn't really about pantries. Those dishes, says Paul, are people. So when you are clean, what are you ready to do (verse 21)?

INSIGHT "Cleanses himself from the latter" is weird language, but it's clear that Christians who are scrubbed clean are handy however God wants to put them to use. It's also clear that you have a choice about whether you're finely shined gold or a lump of clay. Here's one way to read verse 21, again from the New Living Translation: "If you keep yourself pure, you will be a utensil God can use for his purpose. Your life will be clean, and you will be ready for the Master to use you for every good work."

If your goal is to be useful, here's how that happens. What should you flee (verse 22)?

What should you chase (verse 22)?

And who should you chase all that with?

SIDELIGHT Second Timothy 3:2–5 fills out what it looks like when people wander from God. The stuff you're to flee isn't all sex, drugs, and brain-rotting rock and roll. Evil looks pretty every-dayish: "People will be lovers of themselves, lovers of money, boastful, proud, abusive, disobedient to their parents, ungrateful, unholy, without love, unforgiving, slanderous, without self-control, brutal, not lovers of the good, treacherous, rash, conceited, lovers of pleasure rather than lovers of God—having a form of godliness but denying its power."

BIG QUESTIONS Paul might sound to you like a wheezing geezer picking on the chronologically challenged, namely *you*. But why does Paul talk about "evil desires of youth"?

SIDELIGHT Not everything you naturally want is evil. But growing up is *the* time to follow God for yourself, setting your heart on wanting and being the best. Just so you know the adults in the Bible aren't stupid, check out Proverbs 2:1–5. It puts some "back-when-I-was-your-age" stuff like this:

> My son, if you accept my words and store up my commands within you, turning your ear to wisdom and applying your heart to understanding, and if you call out for insight and cry aloud for understanding, and if you look for it as for silver and search for it as for hidden treasure, then you will understand the fear of the Lord and find the knowledge of God.

And if you get that kind of wisdom, Proverbs says, "You will understand what is right and just and fair—every good path. For wisdom will enter your heart, and knowledge will be pleasant to your soul" (Proverbs 2:9–10). That doesn't sound too dumb.

But back to Timothy. Imagine you're Tim. You've received what might be the last words you'll ever hear from your spiritual mentor. He's telling you to flee the evil desires of youth, pursue righteousness, and hang tight with Christian friends. Got the picture? Then apply it to you. Name three things you are fleeing:

Name three points of spiritual growth you are pursuing:

And now name three people "who call on the Lord out of a pure heart" who are helping you run faster:

DEEP THOT If you want to keep growing in God, you've got three tasks: Flee evil. Pursue God and his goodness. And find friends to do it with.

STICKY STUFF Second Timothy 2:22 is crazed, Jesus-followin' stuff to slip into your head. Don't forget the card in back.

ACT ON IT Decide with two or three friends—or even one—what you are going to do to keep getting closer to God.

DIG ON Read Ephesians 4:11–16 to see how much you need those friends to chase God with. No one wants to be a bobbing baby.

Talk About It • 5

EMPATHIZE: What's going on in your life?
ENCOURAGE: How are you doing with Jesus?
EQUIP: What one truth will you take home today?

- How do you expect your faith and obedience to get bigger and stronger? What does God do in you—and what do you do? (Study 21)
- What's the Holy Spirit got to do with you growing? (Study 21)
- Why do you buy the Bible? What do you say to people who don't? (Study 22)
- How do facts and faces make the Bible believable? (Study 22)
- Name three things you would say to someone who asks "Why do you believe in God?" or "Why do you follow Jesus? What evidence could you offer from how you live? (Study 23)
- Have you ever made someone mad by sharing your faith minus the "gentleness and reverence"? What happened? (Study 23)
- How could you use problem-solution-response to tell a friend about Jesus? (Studies 7 and 23)
- Is following Jesus the popular path among the people you know? Please x-plain. (Study 24)
- What's the difference between building on rock—or sand? Which are you doing? (Study 24)
- How are you going to keep getting closer to God now that you've finished *Get God*? What are you ditching? What are you chasing? Who are you chasing it with? (Study 25)

STRAIGHT TALK

BOOKS FOR YOUR GROWING FAITH

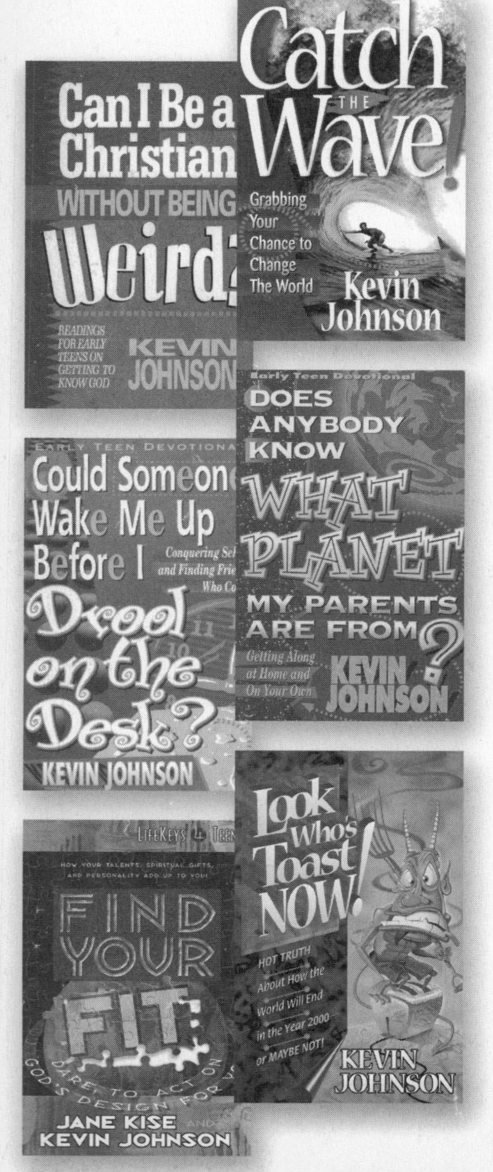

CAN I BE A CHRISTIAN WITHOUT BEING WEIRD?
A series of devotional readings to excite young teens to make Bible reading and prayer a habit by making Scripture understandable and relevant.

CATCH THE WAVE!
An engaging guide to involve teens with God's work in the world. Explores how prayer, ministry at church, school, and around the world can be used by teens to discover the bigness of God's plan.

COULD SOMEBODY WAKE ME UP BEFORE I DROOL ON THE DESK?
Addressing the ups and downs of school and the need to find friends who count, this collection of devotions will point young teens to God as they navigate the tricky path through middle school and beyond.

DOES ANYBODY KNOW WHAT PLANET MY PARENTS ARE FROM?
A fresh look at the homelife of early teens, this collection of readings explores how young adults can make friends at home, walk smart when their parents aren't around, and choose to follow Jesus.

FIND YOUR FIT
Based on the LifeKeys guides to self-discovery, this book provides interactive questions, inventories, and exercises for teens to better understand their talents, skills, and spiritual gifts as they look toward the future.

LOOK WHO'S TOAST NOW!
Answers for teens' insatiable curiosity about the future—the end of the world, death, hell, and Satan. Provides the hope that teens need in this chaotic world and motivation to live holy, patient lives now.

stress*family friction

FROM KEVIN JOHNSON

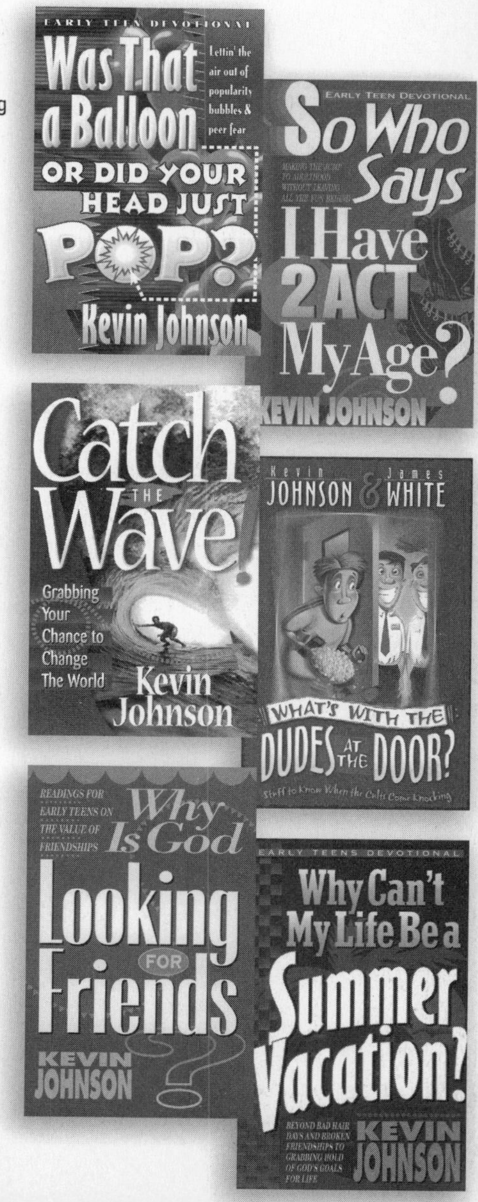

SO WHO SAYS I HAVE TO ACT MY AGE?

Written in acknowledgment that young teens are often caught between being kids and being adults, this group of devotions helps readers understand the inevitable changes that come with growing up.

WAS THAT A BALLOON OR DID YOUR HEAD JUST POP?

A collection of 45 readings that provides the tools for early teens to break free from peer fear, get past put-downs and crowd control, find real popularity with God, and grow into a friend worth having.

WHAT'S WITH THE DUDES AT THE DOOR?

A revealing and alerting teen-friendly look at the major cults. An invaluable tool that provides biblical answers to the key teachings of Mormonism, Jehovah's Witnesses, and other major cults.

WHO SHOULD I LISTEN TO?

This group of readings helps early teens hear God's voice about the pressure-packed roar of the world and gives biblical wisdom to guide them in discerning truth from lies.

WHY CAN'T MY LIFE BE A SUMMER VACATION?

Addressing problems both major and minor—broken friendships to bad hair days—this collection of readings teaches early teens that God provides patient support to help them attain what He has planned for them.

WHY IS GOD LOOKING FOR FRIENDS?

In the language of young teens, this book examines and affirms their longing for friendships that reflects the core of our human nature as God created us.